D1327613

Willa Cather's Modernism

Willa Cather's Modernism

A Study of Style and Technique

Jo Ann Middleton

Rutherford • Madison • Teaneck
Fairleigh Dickinson University Press
London and Toronto: Associated University Presses

Associated University Presses
440 Forsgate Drive
Cranbury, NJ 08512

Associated University Presses
25 Sicilian Avenue
London WC1A 2QH, England

Associated University Presses
P. O. Box 488, Port Credit
Mississauga, Ontario
Canada L5G 4M2

The paper used in this publication meets the requirements
of the American National Standard for Permanence of Paper
for Printed Library Materials Z39.48-1984.

Library of Congress Cataloging-in-Publication Data

Middleton, Jo Ann, 1945–
    Willa Cather's modernism : a study of style and technique / Jo Ann
Middleton.
        p.   cm.
    Includes bibliographical references.   2120 7496
    ISBN 0-8386-3385-4 (alk. paper)
    1. Cather, Willa, 1873–1947—Style.   2 Cather, Willa, 1873–1947—
Technique.   3. Modernism (Literature)—United States.   I. Title.
PS3505.A87Z743   1990
813'.52—dc20   89-45407
                                                                              CIP

PRINTED IN THE UNITED STATES OF AMERICA

First, always, for John . . .

. . . and then for John, Jeffrey, and David

Style is how you write, and you write well when you are interested. A writer's own interest in the story is the essential thing. If there is a flash of warmth in him it is repeated in the reader. The emotion is bigger than style.

I don't think there is anything in ideas. When a young writer tells me he has an idea for a story, he means he has had an emotion that he wants to pass on. An artist has an emotion, and the first thing that he wants to do with it is to find some form to put it in, a design. It reacts on him exactly as food makes a hungry person want to eat. It may tease him for years until he gets the right form for the emotion.

—Willa Cather
in an interview with Flora Merrill,
New York World,
25 April 1925

Contents

Preface

Willa Cather's novels have a curious effect on their readers. To illustrate this point, I would like to relate an anecdote that explains the purpose of this study. As I checked out all the books on Willa Cather, several books on modernism, and a few more on style for what seemed like the thousandth time in the past two years, Phyllis Kalb, one of the librarians at the South Orange Public Library, asked me what I was doing. I replied that I was trying to write a study of Willa Cather's literary technique. She then said, "Cather? I haven't read her in a long time, but she stays in people's minds." Willa Cather pays the same tribute to Sarah Orne Jewett's prose in her essay "Miss Jewett":

> It must leave in the mind of the sensitive reader an intangible residuum of pleasure; a cadence, a quality of voice that is exclusively the writer's own, individual, unique. A quality that one can remember without the volume at hand, can experience over and over again in the mind but can never absolutely define, as one can experience in memory a melody, or the summer perfume of a garden.[1]

Cather's own ability to "stay in people's minds" has fascinated me since I first studied her fiction in Merrill Maguire Skaggs's seminar in the spring of 1984. This writer has an uncanny ability to produce in receptive readers intense emotional reactions to her work, and the impact of such reactions remains remarkably constant even among readers who have developed a deep familiarity with the works. For instance, Marilyn Callander, who has just completed her work on Cather's use of fairy tales, points out that she always cries at a certain point in the *Archbishop* no matter how many times she reads the book nor how prepared she may be for its power. The purpose of this study, therefore, is to explore the methods Cather uses to elicit that intense reader response, which makes it possible for her to "stay with" her reader years after the book has been set down.

The first question one must ask is: What is it about a writer's style that gives her staying power? When we begin to look at

Cather's style, we find that there is no specific, clear definition of it nor is there adequate explanation for the reader's intense emotional reaction to the novels, which is the basis of the works' persistent resonance. Therefore, my investigation of Cather's style proceeds necessarily to a discussion of the techniques that produce this apparently effortless, beautifully simple style.

One interesting aspect of Willa Cather's work becomes increasingly clear as we pursue the specific techniques that she uses to involve the reader's imagination in the story. We find that Cather's techniques arise from a sensibility that is surprisingly "modern" for one who has been so closely identified with the nostalgic pioneer West of the past. We can better understand Cather's attitude toward art if we understand her techniques as rooted in a manner of perception, which we have come to call modern. Although she is both similar to and different from those literary figures known as "modernists," her similarities have far too often been ignored.[2] Modernism in this study, therefore, will refer to the outlook that views the world in its complexity, refuses to accept simple or conventional solutions, and then experiments with new answers and radical suggestions. This study will not attempt to prove that Willa Cather should necessarily be numbered among those who consciously sought the designation "modernist," but rather will note those modernist affinities that elucidate her work, keeping in mind the tenets that have differentiated modernism from any other movement once regarded as radical: the exclusion of sentiment and personal feeling from the literary work; selectivity and precision of diction (usually derived from Flaubert's *le mot juste*); and a conscious effort to reject mimesis and to present the work itself as a new creation. Modernist themes of a willed and violent break with the past, technology's impact on culture, and the psychological unconscious all affected style and technique; plots contained discontinuities, the prose echoed mechanistic rhythms, and narrative reflected the stream of conscious and unconscious images found in dreams and nightmares. Although Cather chose not to experiment with stream-of-consciousness techniques, nor mechanistic prose, she did fully explore the possibilities of discontinuity as she developed her technique of juxtaposition and she mastered the poetic use of the reverberating symbol and image. Modernist writers often returned to the past but not to the immediately previous generation; instead, they returned to the past of an exotic primitive culture, or of a classic Greek and Roman myth, as Cather does when she returns to the pre-European, native American past for a heritage, a tradition within which her individual talent can make its place.

Cather's insistence on the importance of what is *not* in the text, as integral to the created whole as the techniques that produce it, also contributes to the emotional impact of her fiction—and thus to its "staying" power. Although this characteristic has been noted and discussed, Cather's use of stringent excision has not been adequately explicated. Little criticism has dealt with the problem of the gaps that occur in the text because existing critical terminology has been inadequate. In this study I propose that we borrow a scientific term, *vacuole*, and use it as a means to demonstrate the various ways in which Cather manipulates the reader through absences. The vacuole's usefulness arises from its scientific doubleness—it appears empty but is not actually empty (though not full); as "empty" it allows a larger structure than might be expected, and as "not-empty" it performs such functions as storage and digestion, which is suggestive for the apparent absences in Cather's work that are nevertheless full of meaning.

Cather's use of the void is inextricably tied to her theory of reader response, a theory that has its roots in the Jamesian-Flaubertian concept of authorial intent but also relies on the receptivity of the "fine" reader. To Cather, the response of the reader to the text is a criterion against which she measures the success of the text as a work of art and of herself as an artist. Therefore, the evocation of an intense reader response is a primary concern in her technical and stylistic development, and the techniques that she uses must be evaluated in terms of their success in eliciting reader involvement. Contemporary reader-response theories differ from traditional critical theories in that they focus on the reader during the process of reading rather than on the text; in this study, our focus is on the author and the creation of the text. Recent study in the mechanics of reader response, however, helps us articulate the intent and effect of Willa Cather's prose. Although Wolfgang Iser approaches the reader from a critical stance quite different from Willa Cather's, his "implied reader" who "embodies all those predispositions necessary for a literary work to exercise its effect"[3] sounds like a near relation to her "fine reader." Iser's discussion of the function of gaps in the literary text also describes Cather's intended artistic purpose.

Examples of both the use of the vacuole and other reader-involving techniques that Cather employs are found in every one of her novels; however, we will look closely at only three: *A Lost Lady* (1923), *The Professor's House* (1925), and *My Mortal Enemy* (1926). These three books, which come at the midpoint of Cather's career, provide ample illustration of those techniques that Cather perfected to stay with the reader; they represent Cather's final working out of the *démeublé* theory, which she practiced throughout her career, and which she elucidated in her essay, "The Novel Démeublé" (1922).

Substantial critical comment has been made on the importance of absence to Cather in terms of biography; her move from Virginia to Nebraska when she was a child of nine has been frequently and thoroughly explored in terms of her work. Indeed, a great deal of scholarship has pertained to Cather's elusive personal life and its impact on her work; even the most recent scholarship explores the relationship between Cather's life and her work in persuasive and penetrating directions. In this study, however, we will limit our discussion of such material to its specific relevance to Cather's literary techniques, because our focus must remain on Cather, the reader, and the voids with which each must deal.

Edith Lewis once made the observation: "Perhaps there are certain advantages for an artist growing up in an empty country, a country where nothing is made and everything is to be made."[4] She, of course, had in mind that which Cather made out of the country. I would suggest that we turn now to that which Willa Cather made for her reader out of the emptiness.

Acknowledgments

In "148 Charles Street," Willa Cather acknowledged her debt to Mrs. James T. Fields for filling in the gaps in her literary background. Recalling an occasion when Mrs. Fields referred to John Donne, Cather wrote: "I never pretended to Mrs. Fields—I would have had to pretend too much. 'And who,' I brazenly asked, 'was Dr. Donne?' I knew before morning. She had a beautiful patience with Bœotian ignorance, but I was strongly encouraged to take two fat volumes of Dr. Donne to bed with me that night."

I find that my own debt to those who have helped me is substantial, and I am delighted to acknowledge here the community of scholars who have had the patience to overlook my ignorance, fill in many gaps, and encourage me in my work.

I note with appreciation the assistance of Jacqueline Berke of Drew University, who loves E. B. White as I do and who insists on "coherence, coherence, coherence," and Judith L. Johnston of Rider College, whose valuable comments kept this study in focus. To Marilyn Berg Callander and Barbara Caspersen, for their perceptive comments and refreshing common sense, I say thank you. My heartfelt appreciation must also go to my sister, Carole Elisabeth Chaski, who took the time to explain to me the correspondence between my "vacuole" and the unfamiliar realm of linguistics and semantics as she completed her own doctoral work at Brown University.

I am deeply grateful for the perception, encouragement, and generosity of spirit with which Merrill Maguire Skaggs directed the major part of this study as my doctoral dissertation. I must also mention my debt to Sr. Eileen O'Gorman, R.S.C.J., of Manhattanville College, who fostered in me a deep love of American letters over twenty years ago, and who read the manuscript with a kindly and critical eye. I want to express special thanks to James Woodress for his tactful suggestions, his generous support, and his scholarly advice.

I would be remiss if I did not thank the staffs of the Rose Memorial Library, Drew University; the McLaughlin Library,

Seton Hall University; the Dinand Library, Holy Cross College; the Houghton Library, Harvard University; and the South Orange Public Library, for assisting me in my research. I am also grateful to Carolyn Sheehy for permission to refer to letters written by Willa Cather in two collections at The Newberry Library. Special thanks go to Joan Webster, who searched for material in Chicago; to Tara Matthews and Ted Matthews, who tracked down information at Holy Cross; and to John R. Middleton, Jr., who located and verified facts at Harvard.

In addition, I would like to thank Marylee and Milton Chaski for their continued confidence that I would finish this study; Lauren Lepow for her gracious introduction to the world of publishing and for her help in stylistic matters big and small; Yasuko and Paul Grosjean for their help with the word processor; and Esther Conley Middleton, who sent me back to school.

Willa Cather was right when she insisted on the significance of what could not be found in the text. There are no words to express the depth of my gratitude to my family for their part in this project. I thank John for vision, Jeffrey for song, and David for joy. But, most of all, I thank my husband John for always feeling and understanding "the inexplicable presence of the thing not named."

University of Nebraska Press; also reprinted from *Willa Cather in Person: Interviews, Speeches, and Letters*, selected and edited by L. Brent Bohlke, by permission of University of Nebraska Press, © 1986 by the University of Nebraska Press.

"Point of View in Fiction: The Development of a Critical Concept," by Norman Friedman, *Journal of General Education* VIII (1955), 241–53, reprinted by permission of the Penn State Press.

"Restlessness Such as Ours Does Not Make For Beauty," by Rose C. Feld, 21 December 1924 Book Review, © 1924 by The New York Times Company. Reprinted by permission.

"The Vision of a Successful Fiction Writer," by Ethel M. Hockett and "Willa Cather," by Eleanor Hinman, reprinted by permission of the *Lincoln Star*.

"How Willa Cather Found Herself" by Eva Mahoney, reprinted by permission of the *Omaha World-Herald*.

"Willa Cather Raps 'Sincerity Heresy,'" by Harold Small, reprinted by permission of the *San Francisco Chronicle*.

Willa Cather's Modernism

Introduction

In 1949, two years after Willa Cather's death, Katherine Anne Porter wrote about the 1922 Pulitzer Prize winner:

> ... she became a "classic" in her lifetime, and then—well, let me speak only from my own experience in the past two years among students in colleges and universities, mainly students of writing: not one had heard well of her, and not one had read a whole book of hers.[1]

Porter offers no reason for this lack of regard for Cather's work among her colleagues and students. She suggests, however, that the fault lies with a generation of readers who have "trained too much on violence and tricks of doubling and crossing."

When *Sixteen Modern American Writers* was published in 1974, Willa Cather was the only women to be included. At that time, Bernice Slote commented on the paradox of Willa Cather's respected artistry juxtaposed with her relative obscurity. Slote also pointed out the ironies in Cather's career: she had published six novels by 1918, but most of the formal criticism began about 1920; and her most popular fiction remained the Western or pioneer novels she wrote before 1918, even though she wrote many different kinds of fiction during her long, productive life. Slote maintains:

> Even yet, there has been a minimum of formalist criticism, perhaps for two reasons: (1) by the time the New Critics gave attention to the texts of novels as well as of poems, Willa Cather seemed well defined as the Novelist-of-the-Pioneer-Turned-Escapist who looked back with nostalgia to a heroic lost past; and (2) her books had an apparent simplicity and clarity that seemed not to make intellectual demands.[2]

George Greene agrees that we find infrequent references to Cather among the formalists, and "when a judgment is advanced its customary intent is to minimize her importance, to suggest

19

that, within severely circumscribed limits, she has given us modest fictions which are seriously weakened by her incapacity to face modern reality and by a repetitious inclination to idealize the past."[3] Edward Wagenknecht points out that "compared to Joyce or Faulkner or even Henry James, Willa Cather does not seem like a difficult writer. Yet there have been some extraordinary misconceptions about her. She is, we are told, the historian of the Nebraska frontier. And though her workmanship is exquisite, her range is narrow."[4] The designation of regional writer, coupled with a deceptive simplicity of style, served to relegate Cather to a relatively minor role in the development of American literature.[5]

A recent article on minimalism in the *New York Times Book Review* dwells on the contributions of early twentieth-century writers to the movement but perpetuates this injustice by citing Hemingway's theory of writing without mentioning Cather's essay, "The Novel Démeublé," in which she defines the technique.[6] In another such instance, when Reynolds Price considers androgyny in fictional point of view, he discusses significant writers of the eighteenth, nineteenth, and twentieth centuries who wrote in the voice of the opposite gender. Among others, he mentions Tolstoy's Natasha, Flaubert's Emma, and Joyce's Molly as successful examples of the male entering into the female consciousness and cites Emily Brontë's Heathcliff as the only "salient" example of a male consciousness fully realized by a female writer. He mentions Jane Austen, George Eliot, Virginia Woolf, Mary Shelley, and Katherine Anne Porter in his article, listing them with other great artists, both men and women, who lay claim to the tradition of creative androgyny.[7] But nowhere in his discussion is any mention of Willa Cather, perhaps the most successful female creator of male sensibility in American letters. Her perceptive rendering of figures such as Jim Burden, Niel Herbert, Archbishop Latour, and Godfrey St. Peter has not only made them memorable to her readers but has actually generated considerable discussion as to her own sexual orientation. We must ask why Willa Cather does not automatically come to mind in the context of the great literary artists, both men and women, who have created memorable characters of the opposite sex.

Reynolds Price provides only one example of critical blindness to Willa Cather's extraordinary experiments with point of view. Routinely, Cather's innovations, and their possible influence on her younger contemporaries, have been ignored or denigrated. Once the social critics of the 1920s and 1930s categorized Cather as simplistic and nostalgic, her destiny was to be neglected in favor of what they considered more "pertinent" work. Cather herself was content to continue writing for her own artistic satisfaction, trying new ways of reproducing life in art that would evoke for her readers an intense realization and experience of that art. Katherine Anne Porter notes that Cather has a problem in terms of audience; Bernice Slote correctly suggests that the problem lies in Cather's identification as a regional writer and in the all-too-successful and simple style that makes such an identification all too easy. Merrill Maguire Skaggs explains:

> Indeed, her stripping her narratives to their simplest story line and her pure (that is, undecorated) style, plus her consequent accessibility to the average reader, sometimes leave critics nonplussed. Cather's fictions arrive in the hard absoluteness of a very simple polished stone form; each work appears to provoke scarcely more comment than, "What a beautiful sculpture." After mentioning line, balance, smoothness and rhythm, one feels the words which can apply are exhausted.[8]

In this study, we will consider the perfectly executed style that makes Cather's books so deceptively simple to read and so exasperatingly difficult to explain; we will examine the experimental techniques and attitudes that tie Cather to modernism and that result in Cather's own particular form of minimalism, the démeublé style. With the help of a new critical term, the vacuole, we will be better able to understand Catherian absences. In addition, we will demonstrate that Cather's work—using specific practices designed to elicit reader response such as placement of vacuoles, careful juxtaposition of details, concretized form, and complex imagery—requires more from the reader than the "violent and double-crossing" generation might have been willing to invest. The theoretical chapters will be followed by illustrative chapters dealing with three central novels written while Cather was particularly concerned with these techniques: *A Lost Lady*, *The Professor's House*, and *My Mortal Enemy*. The process of writing these three novels, culminating in *My Mortal Enemy*, the most démeublé of Cather's books, ultimately freed Cather for further experimentation in her work. The techniques she perfected in these three novels became as integral a part of that celebrated simple and clear style as her use of color, adverbs, and figures of speech—a style to be felt by the sensitive reader as an emotional experience and recalled with pleasure again and again.

1

The Mystery of Style: Some Keys to Willa Cather's "Calm, Pure Art"

In "Generative Grammars and the Concept of Literary Style," Richard Ohmann states simply: "A style is a way of writing—that is what the word means. And that is almost as much as any-one can say with assurance on the subject, which has been remarkably unencumbered by theoretical insights."[1] In other words, Ohmann offers no explanation for that which we call style other than to assert that style exists. His point is well illus-trated in critical discussions of Willa Cather's work.

Everyone who has an opinion on Willa Cather agrees that she wrote *Alexander's Bridge* in an imitative style; Henry James and Edith Wharton lurk beneath the surface, as well as Edgar Allan Poe and Henry Adams.[2] It is easy to understand why the individualistic Cather did not like the book very much in her later years. It is even easier to use her predecessors and contem-poraries to define its style; all critics conversant with American letters are familiar with the signature styles of James and Whar-ton and Poe and Adams. To define style in these terms, however, is to give no real definition at all.

It is generally agreed among critics that with *O Pioneers!* Willa Cather had found her own style and that she continued to perfect that smooth, precise use of language, imagery, and detail with each succeeding book.[3] Everyone who has an opinion about Willa Cather also concurs that her style is matchless in its clarity, beauty, and simplicity. For instance, Harlan Hatcher calls her work "firm and finely wrought in one of the most satisfactory prose styles for pure clarity and precision in contemporary use.[4] Philip Gerber says that her "premeditated effort to refine her lan-guage, to purify it, resulted in the creation of an instrument at once subtle, evocative, and flexible."[5] Marion Marsh Brown and Ruth Crone summarize:

But on one phase of Willa Cather's art—her style—critics have agreed wholeheartedly. Intangible as style is, there is ample evidence that hers can be termed fine, artistic, beautiful and even classical. It is economical, controlled, and disciplined, refined and fastidious, clear and sharp. . . . Her style is never an end in itself, but always a fitting implement.[6]

Although Brown and Crone are not as vague as Ohmann, here again we find ourselves facing the problem of the intangibility of style.[7]

Cather herself dealt with the problem of defining a particular style in her essay on Katherine Mansfield:

The qualities of a second-rate writer can easily be defined, but a first-rate writer can only be experienced. It is just the thing in him which escapes analysis that makes him first-rate. One can catalogue all the qualities that he shares with other writers, but the thing that is his very own, his timbre, this cannot be defined or explained any more than the quality of a beautiful speaking voice can be.[8]

Willa Cather has a characteristic manner of expression, which we can recognize as clear, beautiful, and simple, and also achieves originality and excellence in her literary expression; these qualities we can catalog. As William Curtin reminds us, however, "Like most of the writers who gained fame during the twenties, Willa Cather was marked by one outstanding characteristic—her individualism."[9] This individualism gave rise to the inexplicable, particular timbre of her style.

In *Poetries and Sciences*, I. A. Richards offers a different perspective. He says that "the poet's style is the direct outcome of the way in which his interests are organized. That amazing capacity of his for ordering speech is only a part of a more amazing capacity for ordering his experience."[10] For Richards, then, style becomes not only a way of ordering language but also a way of ordering experience that is unique to the individual. We might take Richards's definition a step further and suggest that the amazing capacity for ordering both speech and experience is an aptitude and sureness with regard to literary technique that can produce dazzling results when combined with artistic sensibility, genius, and the willingness to experiment. Willa Cather's art arises from her experience of life; her techniques are the result of substantial experimentation through which she discovered the way to order her memories of that experience. Ultimately, then, her style is what she made of her life.

Willa Cather told Latrobe Carroll that "I think that most of the basic material a writer works with is acquired by the age of fifteen."[11] Interestingly enough, with the exception of *Alexander's Bridge, Death Comes for the Archbishop* and *Shadows on the Rock*, the novels are, in fact, drawn from her own experiences before she turned fifteen. Indeed, Cather makes a great point of her unlikely material, particularly in discussing the success of *O Pioneers!*, but we must consider what she does with those childhood memories to understand what she was doing artistically. When Cather said that art was cremated youth, she rightly described the process by which she burned away extraneous details from her childhood memories so that only those that were significant and telling remained to her creative imagination. Her own explanation of the process by which the writer transforms his or her personal experience into literature draws heavily on analogy with other forms of art. In "Miss Jewett" she says:

> The artist spends a lifetime in pursuing the things that haunt him, in having his mind "teased" by them, in trying to get these conceptions down on paper exactly as they are to him and not in conventional poses supposed to reveal their character; trying this method and that, as a painter tries different lightings and different attitudes with his subject to catch the one that presents it more suggestively than any other.[12]

In her essay on *Shadows on the Rock*, Cather uses a musical analogy to explain what she attempted to do in the book: "I took the incomplete air and tried to give it what would correspond to a sympathetic musical setting; tried to develop it into a prose composition not too conclusive, not too definite."[13] And James Woodress records Cather's comparison of the pioneer women of the divide—and of her childhood experience—to the artist:

> Cather always believed that the pioneer women on the Divide possessed many of the traits of the artist—the drive, the perception, the energy, the creative force. They had created a new country out of an idea, just as Fremsted created the roles of Elsa, Seiglinde, Brunhilde or Kundry out of her mind and throat.[14]

Drive, perception, energy, and creative force are the traits of the artist that Cather perceived—and it is as an artist that she wished to perceive herself. Our understanding of what Cather has done with style must therefore be inextricably tied to her concept of artist; our discussion of her techniques hinges on the artistic effects they produce.

Returning to Richards's definition of style, we note that he draws a direct relationship between the style of a particular writer and "the way in which his interests are organized."[15] For this point to shed light on Cather's work, we must look at her interests. It has been established by Cather's biographers that as a child and adolescent she was interested in a wide range of topics from medicine to drama; it has also been well noted that she was most interesting to her neighbors and acquaintances in Red Cloud and Lincoln. The extensive studies of her early journalistic work have established that she maintained her natural curiosity and wrote about a wide variety of subjects in those apprentice years.[16]

Much has been made of the differences between her early, rather ornate, style and the later, much acclaimed, simple style. It seems obvious that Cather must have undergone a considerable change when she left Nebraska for Pittsburgh, and then again when she left Pittsburgh for New York, and finally when she left New York for the territory of her own psyche. However, as we find in many obvious instances, this is not exactly the case. In fact, Bernice Slote posits a convincing case for exactly the opposite viewpoint, maintaining in *The Kingdom of Art* that Cather's interests and attitudes remained constant throughout her life:

What was she like when she left Nebraska? The young Willa Cather—as she is revealed in her writings of the mid-nineties—was primarily a romantic and a primitive. That she was eventually to be called a classicist, a Jamesian sophisticate, and the reserved stylist of the novel démeublé, may be one of the great jokes of literary criticism, for even if the novelist at the age of fifty was different from the beginner of twenty, the critical stages of the years tended to obscure the reality of Cather's work, what was constant in her from those earliest years.[17]

To understand what Slote is talking about, we must identify those interests that remain constant throughout Cather's creative life. The way she organized these interests—that is, her style—necessarily changed as she came to perfect those techniques that best allowed her to make something which "belongs to Literature."[18]

Although Willa Cather disparaged her early work, including

her poetry, many of her stories, and her first novel *Alexander's Bridge*, she does not disparage the apprenticeship that she served as a journalist. Indeed, one finds in her essays an appreciation for those years she spent as critic, reporter, and editor, because from that experience came the ability to discern the difference between mere writing and art. And we feel that she regards these years as necessary for the development of a particular way of seeing one's material. Cather's decision to leave *McClure's* and concentrate on serious writing came about as a result of a letter from Sarah Orne Jewett suggesting that Cather would dissipate her creative energy unless she found her "own quiet centre of life." The older woman's advice proved to be just what Cather needed as a catalyst for her artistic maturation. It is interesting to see Cather reflect on the same catalytic action in another, younger woman's artistic life. She points out that Katherine Mansfield found her "realist self" after her brother's death, when she realized that she too should write from the center of her being and refrain from the showy quality in the early stories. Her brother had brought to her "the New Zealand of their childhood, and out of these memories her best stories were to grow." Cather continues:

> But she did not find too late the things she cared for most. She could not have written that group of New Zealand stories when she first came to London. There had to be a long period of writing for writing's sake. The spontaneous untutored outpouring of personal feeling does not go very far in art. It is only the practised hand that can make the natural gesture,—and the practised hand has often to grope its way.[19]

If we were to substitute "Nebraska" for "New Zealand" and "New York" for "London," the entire passage could refer to Cather's own experience. Mildred Bennett comments on the extraordinary amount of "writing for writing's sake" that Cather did in her journalistic years:

> An impressive, even startling, feature of Willa Cather's journalistic writings is their quantity. As an undergraduate she managed to turn out an astonishing number of Sunday columns, reviews, and articles; and during her five most active years as a newspaperwoman she must have averaged well over a quarter of a million words annually. In comparison with the economy of the later canonical writings— such distillations as *A Lost Lady*, *My Mortal Enemy* and *Sapphira*— this torrent of words points up a major difference between Willa

Cather in the first decade of her career and Willa Cather in the years of her artistic maturity.[20]

As early as 1896, Cather maintained that "journalism has its faults and they are many, but it is considerably nearer to the living world than a university and it has this great merit, that it speedily kills off inferior talent and brings the real article to the front."[21] For the girl from Red Cloud, then, her work on the newspapers of Lincoln showed her life outside the university and proved that she was "the real article." From the beginning Cather demonstrates an interest in setting limits, in defining boundaries. She tells us that "the especial merit of a good reportorial story is that is shall be intensely interesting and pertinent today and shall have lost its point by tomorrow."[22] In that statement we can hear the cub reporter learning the standards of journalism as well as the voice of the editor enforcing them.

Philip Gerber observes that "Cather's own experiences made her acutely aware of the distinction between the journalist who trains himself to write equally well whatever the subject and the creative artist who can do his best only with subjects of deep personal involvement."[23] In "The Novel Démeublé," Cather says that art does not cross certain boundaries: "If the novel is a form of imaginative art, it cannot be at the same time a vivid and brilliant form of journalism."[24] Cather draws a line between journalism and creative writing. Journalism pertains to the moment at hand: its purpose is to inform a large audience, the material is extrinsic to the writer's imagination, and the reporter's job is to write equally well about any subject. Conversely, the object of creative writing is to produce something lasting from experiences and reactions intrinsic to the writer that can be appreciated by a reflective reader. Cather makes a further distinction between mere creative writing and the art of literature: the creation of literature comes from those concerns closest to a writer's own center of being. In her essay "On the Art of Fiction," she says:

> Writing ought either to be the manufacture of stories for which there is a market demand—a business as safe and commendable as making soap or breakfast foods—or it should be an art, which is always a search for something for which there is no market demand, something new and untried, where the values are intrinsic and have nothing to do with standardized values.[25]

For Cather, writers who do not observe strict limits fail at whatever they attempt. She believes that a clarity of purpose and a distinction between mere reporting and actual art must be the constant concern of artists or they will delude both themselves and, for a time only, the reader. She cautions against accepting popular success—which can come all too easily—as real artistic success:

> I should say the greatest obstacles that writers have to get over are the dazzling journalistic successes of twenty years ago, stories that surprised and delighted by their sharp photographic detail and that were really nothing more than living pieces of reporting. The whole aim of that school was novelty—never a very important thing in art.[26]

When Willa Cather says, "To note an artist's limitations is but to define his talent," she expresses a basic element in her approach to the creation of art. Working within strictly defined limits of subject matter and technique, she came to develop the pure style that we can identify but cannot wholly or adequately define. As Gerber has noted, Cather discovers through her long and prolific apprenticeship that "a reporter can write equally well about everything that is presented to his view, but a creative writer can do his best only with what lies within the range and character of his deepest sympathies."[27] Dorothy Canfield recalls that, even in the early Pittsburgh days, Cather compared the art of writing to the playing of a game of tennis: "One must hit the ball as hard as possible, but . . . be sure to keep it within predetermined lines or boundaries to make a success of it."[28] In "A Chance Meeting," Cather points out the relation between knowing and setting boundaries for oneself and developing a style of one's own when she discusses the differences between Balzac and Flaubert. She says that to appreciate both, readers must learn "that an artist's limitations are quite as important as his powers; that they are a definite asset, not a deficiency; and that both go to form his flavour, his personality, the thing by which the ear can immediately recognize Flaubert, Stendhal, Mérimée, Thomas Hardy, Conrad, Brahms, César Franck."[29] She acknowledges her own false start with *Alexander's Bridge* and admits that the full-blooded style of *The Song of the Lark* was not "natural" to her, pointing out that when she limited herself to a simple treatment of her Nebraska memories, she wrote a book for herself that turned out to be the artistically sound and satisfying *O Pioneers!*

One of Cather's deepest concerns was the facile acceptance of any accomplishment that came too easily. For her, that which was real and had actual value for life as well as art was the result of centuries of tradition, years of quiet contemplation, and, what must have seemed to her, eons of being "teased" by the scenes and details that one could not forget. Although "patient" seems an inappropriate adjective for the ambitious girl who aspired to medicine or the young meat-ax critic of the Lincoln newspapers, patience and struggle become part of Cather's artistic creed. In a 1924 interview with Rose Feld for the *New York Times*, Cather maintains that the very prosperity that allows for a book-reading public in America actually hinders the creation of a truly sensitive, artistic culture. Arguing that struggle and a keen appreciation of the realities of life are necessary for the nurture of genius, she holds out the hope that Americans, like the French whom she admires for their "good sense, deliberation and . . . eagerness for the beautiful," will learn the value of patience and experience. She reflects on the assimilation of new immigrants in American society and asserts that:

> Restlessness such as ours, success such as ours, striving such as ours, do not make for beauty. Other things must come first: good cookery; cottages that are homes, not playthings; gardens; repose. These are first-rate things, and out of first-rate stuff is art made.[30]

This interview is especially relevant to our discussion because it occurs just at the point in Cather's career when she was working out the problems and techniques associated with achieving the *démeublé* style. In 1922, two years earlier, she had written "The Novel Démeublé," her call for the "unfurnished" novel, in which she set the criteria for simplicity in writing. That same year she dared to publish a war novel, suffered the sneers of certain contemporaries and the scorn of certain critics, and then won the Pulitzer Prize that some literary lions thought should certainly have gone to a man. The writing of *A Lost Lady*, the novel she published in 1923, proved to be another challenge in which she struggled with the problem of point of view, incorporated the traditions of her masters, Flaubert and James, and worked out for herself a novel that demonstrated something new evolving from the rich past she had absorbed to perfect her own literary voice. At the time of the interview, she was working on *The Professor's House*, in which, she states here, "there will be no theories, no panaceas, no generalizations. It will be a story about people in a prosperous provincial city in the Middle West.

Nothing new or strange, you see."[31] But the novel that she published in 1925 was, in fact, the most experimental in form and most radical in technique she had written yet. In this book she resolves her struggle to find a significant past out of which a truly American tradition can arise by going back to the ancient Indian civilization, and she juxtaposes the materialistic and "restless" present against this rich, serene culture. As she insists, the book is a story about people, however, and Cather's Professor is the custodian of lasting values in a society that is moving too fast to appreciate them.

In *Shadows on the Rock,* Cather illustrates the making of first-rate things when she shows us Madame Auclair's determination that her daughter know the old ways so that she could maintain a French home and garden in the Canadian wilderness. Here she makes the relationship between those careful housekeeping customs and the moral values of a whole civilization explicit:

> The sense of "our way,"—that was what she longed to leave with her daughter. She wanted to believe that when she herself was lying in this rude Canadian earth, life would go on almost unchanged in this room with its dear (and, to her, beautiful) objects; that the proprieties would be observed, all the little shades of feeling which make the common fine. The individuality, the character, of M. Auclair's house, though it appeared to be made up of wood and cloth and glass and a little silver, was really made up of very fine moral qualities in two women: the mother's unswerving fidelity to certain traditions, and the daughter's loyalty to her mother's wish.[32]

Bishop Latour voices the same belief in *Death Comes for the Archbishop* when he tells Father Vaillant, "I am not deprecating your individual talent, Joseph, . . . but, when one thinks of it, a soup like this is not the work of one man. It is the result of a constantly refined tradition. There are nearly a thousand years of history in this soup."[33]

Willa Cather viewed herself as an American writer and perhaps felt the need to develop something like this "constantly refined tradition" in American letters. If so, then the constant refinement of style that occupies her in her middle years is a legacy and tribute to the hard work, struggle, good sense, discrimination, and an eagerness for beauty that she demanded of herself as well as from others.

Her respect for the traditions and values of the past, however, provides one of the reasons critics dismiss Cather as nostalgic, outdated, or "genteel," to use Lionel Trilling's designation. Granville Hicks accuses Cather of flight into "supine romanticism," adding that "she has preferred the calm security of her dreams, and she has paid the price."[34] And, although Morton Zabel emphasizes that Cather was able to find means of simplification, discipline, and curtailment that would result in the "best books of her best years," he also calls these books "essentially minor in substance" and "elegiac in their version of American history." He concludes that "backwardness was with her not only a matter of her material and temperament. It was the condition of her existence as an artist."[35] The very point on which these critics fault Cather is one of the essential elements of her particular creative drive. They misread the use to which Cather puts the past, not realizing that from this "backwardness" she produces some of the most unheralded literary experiments of the early twentieth century.[36]

Thea's sense of identification with the Ancient People in *The Song of the Lark* frees her to become woman and artist; in Panther Canyon she discovers a heritage from those ancient artisans that teaches her how to create beauty—that is, art—from mere talent. Willa Cather's sense of identification with the past enabled her to create beauty (art) through a distillation of the memories and experiences that made up that past. It took her half her life to assimilate all that would eventually form the basis of her art and when she was ready to give it forth as art it took a deceptively clear and simple form—not unlike the simple soup that contains a thousand years of history.

Two of Cather's overriding concerns throughout her career involve discovering and working within one's limitations, and also discovering one's own particular material within the context of the tradition that has produced one, then putting it down rightly on paper. By constantly attending to these concerns, a writer becomes an artist and, in the process, his or her manner of recording experience becomes a style, the "thing that is his very own, his timbre [which] cannot be defined or explained any more than the quality of a beautiful speaking voice can be." In the next chapter, we shall consider the specific techniques that Willa Cather used to record her experiences as she perfected a style that could indeed create art out of life.

2

The Mastery of Technique: Willa Cather's Fusion of Craftsmanship and Vision

As I have shown in chapter 1, the definition of style is elusive. Therefore, to study Willa Cather's art, we must look for some more easily accessible terms in which to understand what she has done in her novels. Style itself breaks down to certain techniques, certain ways of arranging words; although style is admittedly more than the sum of its techniques, they do provide various aspects of style that we can more easily apprehend. If we look closely at Cather's texts, as John Randall does in *The Landscape and the Looking Glass*, it is "clear from the first that she was a conscious contriver of the smaller units of style, the sentence and the paragraph."[1] Mildred Bennett explains to new students of Cather that her style is derived from her use of color, figurative language, and economy—all elements of technique. Bennett says:

> Cather's method was to write fully, then strip every sentence to its unadorned simplicity. To accomplish this, she eliminated many adverbs, used strong verbs, and many figures of speech. And whenever she felt great emotion, she used color.[2]

Both Randall and Bennett point to specific techniques that produce Cather's unique style and indicate that Cather was acutely aware of the technical side of creative writing. The actual essence of what makes the writing individualistic is still intangible, but the methods of achieving style can be enumerated and studied. *Style* itself evades definition, but *technique*—which encompasses the many ways of writing down the language to communicate an artistic whole from writer to reader—is accessible. A major advantage in studying technique is that its elements can be identified, defined, and taught. Technique bridges the gap between the components of literature and the actual use of those various parts. Plot, character, setting, and theme are inert ingredients; the techniques by which they are assembled produce the art of literature.[3] To fully appreciate a writer's achievement, therefore, it would seem imperative to examine the techniques that structure his or her work.

As Thomas Uzzell says, "technique is a way to lucidity. It is a study of the thinking processes of the writer, which of course explains its unpopularity. The reward is the ability to think clearly although inspired."[4] The way in which writers put thoughts down on paper reflects the way in which they organize their interests; the techniques they use are an indication of the way in which each thinks. One might propose the notion that the techniques a writer uses result from a mental attitude toward both the subject matter at hand and the craft of writing. The thinking processes of the writer must certainly include his or her purpose in undertaking each new work; any discussion of technique must ultimately lead to a consideration of the writer's stance with regard to the reader.

In "Technique as Discovery," Mark Shorer tells us that "the difference between content, or experience, and achieved content, or art, is technique." He continues by explaining:

> For technique is the means by which the writer's experience, which is his subject matter, compels him to attend to it; technique is the only means he has of discovering, exploring, developing his subject, of conveying its meaning, and, finally, of evaluating it.[5]

If we accept I. A. Richards's suggestion that style is the writer's way of organizing his or her interests, then we can readily accept Shorer's notion that technique arises from the writer's experience. For Shorer, a writer takes the raw material of experience and processes it to create art. In doing so, the writer discovers the appropriate technique for dealing with each new set of parameters in each new work of art. Here we recall Cather's discovery that in true art (as in her creation of O Pioneers!), form derives naturally from subject matter. She refers to this realization as an explosion of understanding; Uzzell would analyze what happens by saying that "technique is at work in all that happens from the moment of first inspiration to the completion of the design, and indeed is involved in the actual writing insofar as the writing is a fulfillment of the design."[6] Cather herself explains how content dictates technique in "Miss Jewett" when she discusses the "two kinds of making":

> the first, which is full of perception and feeling but rather fluid and formless; the second, which is tightly built and significant in design. The design is, indeed, so happy, so right, that it seems inevitable; the design is the story and the story is the design.[7]

She continues by telling us how a writer is able to discover the technique by which one can explore, develop, evaluate, and convey the meaning of experience: "If he achieves anything noble, anything enduring, it must be by giving himself absolutely to his material. And this gift of sympathy is his great gift; it is the fine thing in him that alone can make his work fine."[8] For Cather, writers must give themselves over to their work to produce that which can rightly be called art. We are reminded of the image of Thea's throat as a vessel through which her voice could flow, and we must recall Cather's own admonition: "In the kingdom of art there is no God, but one God, and his service is so exacting that there are few men born of women who are strong enough to take the vows."[9] These are strong words—in her inflated journalistic mode—for a novice, but this belief remained one of Cather's steadfast principles throughout her life. For Cather, giving oneself over to the material was one of the great joys of writing; like T. S. Eliot, she did not think of writing as a loss of her personality, but rather "a complete loss of self for three hours a day."[10] In an unpublished dissertation that deals with Cather's technique, Jean Lavon Throckmorton points out that

> it has already been suggested that such a theory of the relation between inspiration and form is perfectly compatible with a firm belief in the need for acquiring technique. It even casts light on what Willa Cather meant when she spoke of "technique"—the skill with which an author was able to capture in actual words that which the unconscious part of the process of creation had given him.[11]

A concern with technique, defined in this manner, is consistent with Cather's interest in defining limits; the fluid and formless kind of making—though it be perceptive—resulted from a lack of internal design. One might compare this kind of writing to her more perceptive newspaper criticism; although she had many interesting insights in her columns, none of these articles could cross the line between the two kinds of writing.

Cather sees artistic limitation as liberating rather than as restricting. In "Light on Adobe Walls," she tells us how she approaches her work:

> The first thing an artist does when he begins a new work is to lay down the barriers and limitations; he decides upon a certain composition, a certain key, a certain relation of creatures or objects to each other. He is never free, and the more splendid his imagination, the more intense his feeling, the farther he goes from general truth and general emotion.[12]

We can understand why Cather disliked "the free-verse bunch from the Middle West" and admired the tight, controlled verses of Robert Frost.[13]

So then, the first technique that we must appreciate is that of defining limits, and it is a technique that arises directly from Cather's own long apprenticeship in the service of art. We might see Cather's idea of the artist as a conduit for creation within artistic limits as an early expression of Gabriel Josipovici's later notion that "art, the making of an artifact, becomes the means whereby the artist frees himself from the shackles of self without disintegrating into chaos."[14] As Edward and Lillian Bloom point out, this technique of setting limits and then giving oneself over totally to the material is not for everyone, though it is essential for the creation of art as Cather defines it:

> Critics and practitioners of the novel may of course take exception to a concept which places such stringent demands upon the writer that his own personality must be absorbed in each work of art, that his own being becomes virtually husk and texture of the novel. . . . A basic element of Miss Cather's great talent, however, was the perception of infinite variations of human mood and aspiration. To enunciate such perception, she had no choice but to participate in each novel, not so much through authorial commentary as through sharing in the feelings of her central characters.[15]

Cather lived with her material for so long that she was able to give herself over to it with the confidence that the appropriate form, or design, of the book would emerge in the act of its creation.[16]

In her memoirs, Fanny Butcher recalls Willa Cather's singular devotion to the purity of literary art, and she brings to our attention an aspect of Cather's work that has often been overlooked or misunderstood:

Nothing could be farther from any kind of literary dishonesty than the writing of Willa Cather. She was never diverted from what she knew was right in her work, by any of the temptations that literary success often brings: money, fame, or the pressure to write another book like its best-selling predecessor. Like all great artists, she experimented—saw and added new dimensions to her work. But she did it with such skill and subtlety that few readers realize how experimental all of her writing was.[17]

Although Edward Wagenknecht accurately says that there have been some "extraordinary misconceptions" about Willa Cather, he persists in perpetuating the misconception that "she shows few signs of having lived through a period when the novel was becoming more and more experimental."[18] David Daiches charges that Cather "could have learned something from the so-called 'stream of consciousness' technique, and from many other experimental devices introduced in the early years of the century" and regrets that she "was not interested in any kind of radical experimentation with the technique of the novel."[19] Elizabeth Shepley Sergeant asks:

Why was someone who sanctioned the modern in painting so removed from the *avant-garde* of literary America or a literary Europe at this time? The young men of *The Seven Arts; The Dial* under Schofield Thayer, even with the discerning Alyse Gregory at the helm, and then the unique Marianne Moore; these ignored her altogether. Willa Cather was not, as the French say, *dans le movement*; the movement had pretty well scrapped the Victorian age which she still idealized. The *avant-garde* were thus as blind to her qualities as she to theirs, though she, too, cared for Proust and saw *Ulysses* as a landmark.[20]

I believe that Sergeant missed the significance of what Willa Cather was quietly doing to the novel. In 1923, the year to which Sergeant refers in the preceding passage, Cather was fifty years old; she had no need or desire to establish herself as one of the avant-garde. By the time she was fifty, Willa Cather had enjoyed separate careers as journalist, critic, teacher, editor, and writer; she had published a volume of poetry, two short story collections, five novels, and had won the Pulitzer Prize. Ahead of her was the best and most experimental work of her career. William Curtin asserts that it would have been "presumptuous" to ask Cather to follow anyone else's path. He says:

She had formed and matured her ideas on art before she wrote a novel. She had no more reason to follow Gertrude Stein and James Joyce, whose work she respected, than they did to follow her. Her style solves the problems in which she was interested. She wanted to stand midway between the journalists whose omniscient objectivity accumulates more fact than any character could notice and the psychological novelist whose use of the subjective point of view stories distorts objective reality.[21]

Aware of her contemporaries and their work, she nevertheless remained aloof, avoiding identification with any particular movement and maintaining that single-minded devotion to her own muse. Perhaps the struggle to establish herself as a woman independent of the large family from which she came and as an artist independent of all obligations other than those that art itself imposed on her resulted in the apparent isolation in which she worked. Ample evidence suggests that, eccentric and independent as she was, she did not practice an intellectual isolation and was familiar with all of the technical innovations and current literary theory of the time.[22]

Why, then, didn't the avant-garde look to Willa Cather, as they did to Gertrude Stein, for guidance and inspiration? First, Cather's work appeared too simple and clear, too easily understood; complexity was integral to the modernists. Second, they must have believed that Cather was too popular a writer to be very good; a certain elitism marked the new breed of writer. Third, Cather's subject matter seemed nostalgic, her style seemed romantic, and her respect for tradition seemed old-fashioned to those revolting against nineteenth-century literary conventions.

Ironically, Willa Cather had tried and succeeded in her own quiet experiments at many of the techniques we now call modern; she had long before made the "modern" attitude toward literature her very own.[23] Sadly enough, Cather is still largely neglected in critical discussions of the innovative figures of early twentieth-century American letters. Perhaps some of this neglect is a result of Cather's own disinterest; certainly some of it is related to the time and place in which she lived. George Schloss nevertheless suggests that

this isolation may have been fortunate. It forced her to go her own way and permitted her to become both a bridge between the best and a counter-irritant against the worst aspects of both periods. Perched between two eras she could see the true and false in each; though unhappily, in the press of the "new writing," her own best work, produced between 1918–1931, was passed over by the "revolutionaries" whom it might have benefited most.[24]

In the Feld interview of 1924, Cather remarked:

> The world goes through periods or waves of art. Between these periods come great resting places. We may be resting right now. Older countries have their wealth of former years to fall back upon. We haven't. But, like older countries, we have a few individuals who have caught the flame of former years and are carrying the torch into the next period. Whistler was one of these, Whitman was another.[25]

Willa Cather appears to be one of the individuals who carry the torch from one great period to another. E. K. Brown notes the difficulties in relating Cather's work to either the psychoanalytical explorations of the 1920s or the sociological inquiries of the 1930s, but he asserts that one can make connections:

> It was amid the technical enthusiasms of the Twenties that Miss Cather developed a new method of narration and a new use of setting, shaking off all the heaviness and dullness of the traditional novel as she had formerly conceived it and as most of her contemporaries continued to practice it. Her fiction has its sociology: she broke off her history of the decay of the small Mid-Western town just where Sinclair Lewis began his.[26]

Although Cather's contemporaries exhibited a certain blindness to her accomplishments, we have the historical perspective to examine her modernity in terms of both her artistic theories and her actual practice of those theories. In *The Modern Tradition: Backgrounds of Modern Literature*, Richard Ellmann and Charles Feidelson, Jr., demonstrate that modernism itself arises from a long tradition of speculative enterprise, saying that "it is clear that 'modern' amounts to more than a chronological description. The term designates a distinctive kind of imagination—themes and forms, conditions and modes of creation, that are interpreted and comprise an imaginative whole."[27] Irving Howe proposes that the modern refers to "sensibility and style":

> The modern must be defined in terms of what it is not, the embodiment of a tacit polemic, an inclusive negative. Modern writers find that they begin to work at a moment when culture is marked by a

prevalent style of perception and feeling; and their modernity consists in a revolt against this prevalent style, an unyielding rage against the official order. But modernism does not establish a prevalent style of its own; or, if it does, it denies itself, thereby ceasing to be modern. . . . It becomes a condition of being a writer that he rebel, not merely and sometimes not all against received opinions, but against the received ways of doing the writer's work.[28]

Cather's rebellion against the naturalistic method of writing, her willingness to let content dictate form, her faith in the suggestiveness of literature, and her insistence on exacting techniques that lead to simplicity of style indicate a modernist sensibility; we now have the historical perspective to make that judgment.

Although it is not my purpose here to classify Willa Cather as a member of some modernist school—she is much too independent a thinker even for that designation—it is productive to examine her attitudes toward art as they align with those we generally accept as modernist, and how frequently her own experiments anticipate or coincide with the achievements of such writers as Joyce, Proust, Eliot, or Pound.

The creation of a new novel form is one of the major preoccupations of modernist writers, those artists of the early twentieth century who sought new directions for art in order to address what they perceived as a new and more complex world. It is generally agreed that the most influential figures of the movement are the great experimenters like Proust, Cézanne, and Joyce, all of whom were known to Cather. Josipovici says:

> But what is Modernism? As I understand it the word refers to that revolution in the arts which took place between 1880 and 1920 and which we associate with the names of Cézanne, Mallarmé, Proust, Joyce, Kafka, Eliot, Schoenberg, Stravinsky, Picasso and Kadinsky.[29]

Harold Fickett and Douglas R. Gilbert identify the years of "Modernism proper" as 1915 to 1941 and list as the great works of that period James Joyce's *Ulysses* and Ezra Pound's *Cantos*.[30] David Craig calls Pound, Eliot, and Joyce the "leading modernists."[31] Peter Ackroyd, however, attributes the origins of modernism to an earlier and, for Cather, more influential "father":

> The central transition . . . is the emergence of the idea of "literature." It is this idea which separates classical modernism from the modernism of our own time, and it propels us into our own time with a name so familiar that it seems to have no origin. But it does have an

origin—and it also has a history. It first comes into the light, as a conceived entity, in the writing of Gustave Flaubert. He is the first modern writer to detach his "presence" from his own writings, so that
the language sustains itself with its own weight.[32]

Cather's assimilation of the literary standards of Flaubert was
coupled with her close attention to the critical essays of Henry
James in which, as Peter Faulkner observes, he "showed an intense interest in the technical problems of the novelist's art."
Faulkner adds that "this theoretical concern running alongside
the practice of art was itself to be characteristic of Modernism."[33]
Willa Cather trained on the two masters in whom modernism
germinated; it is no wonder that we can find in her work those
characteristics that mark the modern. From Flaubert, she learned
the value of language, the beauty of the well-made sentence, and
the power of selective detail; from James, she learned the necessity of suggestion, the importance of compression, and the evocation of emotion. To these she added her own criteria of limitation
and patience in order to process her memories into art, and her
own willingness to experiment in order to find the right technique to do so.

   In "The Theory of the Novel," Philip Stevick states that we
must make two assumptions when we discuss technique:

> The first of these is that techniques have no existence apart from
> their employment in particular novels, that one cannot begin to judge
> the effectiveness of one way of telling a story over another without
> judging the relation between that technique and the whole structure
> of the novel in which it appears. A theory of technique also requires
> that the critic assume that the subject matter of a novel—its ideas,
> its themes, its systems of values—cannot be separated from its tech-
> nique, since it is only by means of technique that these themes and
> values have any existence at all.[34]

This statement may sound like mere repetition of the point that
content and technique are mutually dependent—and produce a
distinctive style. We must emphasize, however, Stevick's point.
Each work of fiction stands as a completed, made thing. Therefore, each work of Cather's must be judged on its own terms; each
must be assessed as to the effectiveness of the techniques that
she used to express the content. Although Cather's style has certain characteristics, such as classical simplicity, clarity, and
beauty, which are easily recognizable throughout the whole oeu-

vre, and although we can identify certain techniques in every novel, we must acknowledge that each book is different from every other; the difference lies in the unique combination of subject matter and technique she devised for each new foray into the great kingdom of art.

According to Webster, the word *experiment* means "a test or trial of something; specifically . . . any action or process undertaken to discover something not yet known or demonstrate something known."[35] The purpose behind each of Cather's books is to discover a way of representing experience in language, and, for each experience, the way is unique. As noted earlier, Cather is aware that not every trial is successful, but that each is necessary for the writer in pursuit of art: "And at the end of a lifetime he emerges with much that is more or less happy experimenting, and comparatively little that is the very flower of himself and his genius."[36] Cather sees experimentation as integral to creation, and this attitude makes her modern. As Lillian Bloom reminds us:

> Never did she experiment for its own sake. When experimentation was dictated by the need to reconcile concept and form, it was but one more way in which she could infuse her novel with a quiet, unobtrusive sympathy.[37]

Cather actively tried a new approach with each book, and each book dictated its own experiment. Even though *Alexander's Bridge* is structurally symmetrical—a "studio picture"—we can appreciate Cather's efforts to involve her reader on several levels. For instance, the carefully chosen images that tie it to Poe's "The Fall of the House of Usher" enhance and deepen the reader's response to the novel.[38] *O Pioneers!* is an experiment in subject matter and form; James Schroeter observes that the very fact of using immigrants was avant-garde.[39] *The Song of the Lark* is the experiment in the "full-blooded method" and the transformation of biography to art. With *My Ántonia* Cather begins the series of experiments with point of view; *A Lost Lady* and *One of Ours* are also technical masterpieces that resolve the issue of point of view.[40] Indeed, Cather's experiments with point of view are one aspect of her work that ties her so closely to the twentieth-century modernists. As Jonathan Raban points out in *The Technique of Modern Fiction*:

> Recent fiction has been dominated by the theory of the limited point of view. . . . If modern fiction has one overwhelming common theme,

it is that of the conflict between the individual sensibility and the alien world outside. With such a subject only one point of view is possible—that of the sensitive, and usually suffering, hero.[41]

Another example of limited point of view is *My Mortal Enemy*, but perhaps it is better seen as Cather's consummate experiment in the novel *démeublé*, a book so simply and concisely written that it scarcely seems a novel at all—at first glance.

Cather herself refers to two of the books as experimental; she comments on *Death Comes for the Archbishop* by saying that "I had all my life wanted to do something in the style of legend, which is absolutely the reverse of dramatic treatment."[42] She also explains that she set herself two technical problems in *The Professor's House:*

> When I wrote *The Professor's House*, I wished to try two experiments in form. The first is the device often used by the early French and Spanish novelists; that of inserting the *Nouvelle* into the *Roman*. . . . But the experiment which interested me was something a little more vague, and very much akin to the arrangement followed in sonatas in which the academic sonata form was handled somewhat freely.[43]

Both of these books caused the critics no little consternation as they tried to classify them using traditional literary conventions.

When she discusses *Shadows on the Rock*, Cather calls her method "anacoluthon," which, as Edward and Lillian Bloom explain, meant for her the basis of the form she used rather than an academic or cultural stance. They illustrate the manner in which she used the wealth of critical and classical knowledge she had accumulated for her own growth as an artist:

> Classically, the purpose of anacoluthon was to evoke an emotional or moral effect through a temporary suspension of completeness—that is, like a series of minor suspenses—within the individual actions of the principal framework. Once identified, the term has great bearing on the working out of *Shadows*. The seeming disjunction implied by the term she attained by initiating episodes and then disclosing their resolutions in subsequent appropriate phases of the novel. It is an example of Miss Cather's critical density, her tendency to put undefined or meagrely defined theories into esthetic practice.[44]

As the writers of the twentieth century discarded the literary conventions of the nineteenth, they looked for new methods of expression, new forms. Cather reached far back into classical modes to exploit little-used concepts and make them fresh. In *Lucy Gayheart*, she reaches into the not-so-distant past to experiment with the worn-out and hackneyed novel of her own contemporaries. Paul Comeau makes an interesting argument for the novel as a complex, daring experiment; he maintains that the story of Lucy is, in fact, a mirror of what Cather is trying to do in the book. Aware of the traditional nature of Lucy's story, Cather "employs it nevertheless to draw attention to the mighty craft by which foolish old words are given their full value." He says in admiration:

> Clearly, Willa Cather knew the perils of the voyage she was undertaking, just as she knew her limitations as an artist at age 62 (like the old soprano, the original sweetness had gone from her voice), but, as always, she was willing to risk a great deal in the name of experimentation, of artistic integrity.[45]

Because it was vital to her life as an artist, Cather maintained the modern attitude to the end of her career. *Sapphira and the Slave Girl*, which has been written off as a weak novel of her old age, is beginning to impress readers as another bold departure from literary convention. David Stouck asserts that "*Sapphira and the Slave Girl*, with its figurations of life from the viewpoint of a five-year-old child, was as experimental as her first attempt at epic in *Alexander's Bridge* or her use of sonata form in *The Professor's House*."[46] Merrill Maguire Skaggs explores the ease with which Cather stands conventions on their heads and reverses all of her reader's expectations in "Willa Cather's Experimental Southern Novel."[47] Susan Rosowski proposes:

> When we look beyond the antebellum Virginia setting, we realize that Cather's last novel, long dismissed as escapist, may well be the most directly political of all her writing. In its central tension over inaction of characters against the increasingly disturbing and, finally, evil action of a powerful central figure, Cather's novel unexpectedly resembles nothing so much as Thomas Mann's "Mario and the Magician."[48]

Unlike many of the other "experimenters," however, Cather took the path of simplicity rather than that of obscurity. Cather's technical skills are so refined that the works appear too easily read; indeed, simplification may be the key to understanding just what Cather has done to the novel form. In her essay, "On the Art of Fiction," she says:

> Art, it seems to me, should simplify. That, indeed, is very nearly the whole of the higher artistic process; finding what conventions of form and detail one can do without and yet preserve the spirit of the whole—so that all that one has suppressed and cut away is there to the reader's consciousness as much as if it were in type on the page.[49]

In her famous manifesto "The Novel Démeublé," which Fitzgerald acknowledged as influential for his own work,[50] she asserts:

> The higher processes of art are all processes of simplification. The novelist must learn to write, and then he must unlearn it; just as the modern painter learns to draw and then learns utterly to disregard his accomplishment, when to subordinate it to a higher and truer effect.[51]

The process that Cather advocates is not an easy one to learn or to practice, although it has become the minimalist code. As the Blooms observe, "the ability to simplify is not easily acquired, for it comes only with time and a stringent determination to cast out anything that does not contribute to the spirit of the whole."[52]

Mona Pers makes an interesting observation when she says that Willa Cather expresses the way a child reacts to the world: "He senses the overtones in what to adults may seem everyday situations, people and places. She was convinced that the difference in outlook was due to the child's greater power of imagination."[53] To read these books well despite their childlike simplicity, however, is to see the complexity behind them, to sense the overtones that they create. We will explore this aspect of Cather's modernity at a later point when we discuss her relationship to her reader. At present, we must note that this attitude toward writing necessitates a compression of language, a selectivity of significant detail, and the careful use of that detail.

Perhaps one of Willa Cather's most famous statements is that "the world broke in two in 1922 or thereabouts."[54] Most often this is cited as an example of Cather's "backwardness" and used to support the notion that she was nostalgic in her attitude toward the past. Cather's statement, however, is eerily reminiscent of another one made by another female writer and given a totally different interpretation by Richard Freedman. In *The Novel*, Freedman recalls Virginia Woolf's contention that "in or about

December 1910, human character changed." He concludes that "it wasn't human nature that had changed, of course, but rather the novelist's way of perceiving and ordering it."[55] Peter Faulkner points out that the world was thought to be much more complex after 1910;[56] Josipovici cites the crisis of authority in every sphere of activity in the late nineteenth century.[57] Cather says:

> Just how did this change come about, one wonders. When and where were the Arnolds overthrown and the Brownings devalued? Was it at the Marne? At Versailles, when a new geography was being made on paper? Certainly the literary world which emerged from the war used a new coinage. In England and America the "masters" of the last century diminished in stature and pertinence, became remote and shadowy.[58]

If it is the perception and ordering of the world and one's experience in that world that entitles a writer to the designation "modern," then Willa Cather merits that designation. When we attribute to Cather a modern attitude, we mean a way of looking at her experience in terms of the complex world around her and, consequently, the way in which she transforms that personal experience into a work of general significance. Not only does she recognize the increasing complexities of the world, but also deals with them in modern terms. Her definition of a novel incorporates this notion:

> But a novel, it seems to me, is merely a work of imagination in which a writer tries to present the experiences and emotions of a group of people by the light of his own. That is really what he does, whether the method is "objective" or "subjective."[59]

Cather gives equal importance to experience and emotion. For her, a work of art must be able to recreate the emotional component for readers as well as convince them of the authenticity of the experience related. As she said, "One is bumped up smartly against the truth, old enough but always new, that in novels, as in poetry, the facts are nothing, the feeling is everything."[60] This conviction is also expressed in T. S. Eliot's early essays that propose a denial of the self-conscious romantic ideal that poets express themselves and an assertion that the structure and content of the work itself establish meaning and emotion.[61]

Her experience is made clear to her, and ultimately to her reader, through juxtaposition with her understanding of her own—and the larger, historical—past. We have mentioned Cather's sense of history as constituting a continuum out of which the artist emerges. Ellmann and Feidelson state:

> The modernists have been as much imbued with a feeling for their historical role, their relation to the past, as with a feeling of historical discontinuity. They have had an ancestral line, even if it is often an underground stream. Their suspicion of old forms has made them search for kinsmen in old rebellion.[62]

We recall Cather's use of the classical anacoluthon in *Shadows on the Rock*, her use of epic in *Alexander's Bridge*, and her reference to pastoral traditions in *My Ántonia*.

Although one of the accusations against Cather is that she withdrew from modern life in disgust and indulged in nostalgia for a lost and golden past, we can see more clearly today that she merely engaged in a modernist technique of juxtaposing past and present. Stephen Spender discusses this kind of modernist confrontation with the past in his essay "Moderns and Contemporaries":

> The modern is the past become conscious at certain points which we are ourselves "living" in the present. Hence we find that the modern in his work is occupied with trying to bridge a gulf within his own awareness, of past from present. With his sensibility he is committed to the present; with his intellect he is committed to criticizing that present by applying it to his realization of the past. . . . The modern is acutely conscious of the contemporary scene, but he does *not* accept its values. To the modern, it seems that a world of unprecedented phenomena has today cut us off from the life of the past and in doing so from traditional consciousness.[63]

Seen in this light, the pioneer novels comment indirectly on the loss of pioneer values in the modern world, and *A Lost Lady* and *The Professor's House* make direct statements about the standards in the contemporary world that produce a modern alienation from our roots. What we must emphasize is that these works are an expression not of despair but of concern. Cather certainly appears optimistic about the future, even as she deplores the materialism of the present in "Nebraska: The End of the First Cycle" (1923):

> Surely the materialism and showy extravagance of this hour are a passing phase! They will mean no more in half a century from now

than will the "hard times" of twenty-five years ago—which are already forgotten. The population is as clean and full of vigor as the soil; there are no old grudges, no heritages of disease or hate. The belief that smug success and easy money are the real aims of human life has settled down over our prairies, but it has not yet hardened into molds and crusts. The people are warm, mercurial, impressionable, restless, over-fond of novelty and change. These are not qualities which make the dull chapters of history.[64]

For Cather, artists bear a responsibility for creating works that will belong to and be true for all time. It is their duty to see the present in terms of the past; it is their creative imagination that must discern the thing of true worth. George Greene attributes some of the critical indifference to Cather to this very attitude. He says:

> Better than any writer of her era she represented the ideal of the artist as a bringer of truth rather than a reporter of the status quo. Her vision, in its less assertive embodiments, impressed cursory readers as a form of mandarin pride and lowered Miss Cather's stature during her lifetime—giving use to one image of her which still persists.[65]

Cather realizes that understanding and expression are a result of a new way of seeing, which the artist works to develop. Like Woolf, Cather's perception adjusted to accommodate a bifocal vision of the past and the present juxtaposed, and her techniques reflect that adjustment. Eudora Welty suggests that Cather's ability to see things from this perspective was a direct result of her childhood environment. She says that "Willa Cather brought past and present into juxtaposition to the most powerful effect. And the landscape itself must have shown her this juxtaposition. . . . The lack of middle distance may have something to do with the way characters in the foreground cast such long, backreaching shadows."[66] Again we reiterate that all of Cather's experiences became material to be remembered, assimilated, and—ultimately—given forth as art.

Eric Auerbach points out:

> The sense of the almost overwhelming abundance of the experience to be made into art marks off Modernism from the rarefied atmosphere of symbolism and aestheticism. . . . Thus we have the various experiments in method that characterize the development of Modernism in all the arts. Since these all aimed to get beyond the oversimplified accounts of experience which traditional art was held to

give, they necessarily involved new methods of organization, particularly through juxtaposition (rather than simple narration) and irony (rather than unity of mood).[67]

For Cather, juxtaposition is not only a way of perception but also one of the most identifiable techniques in her work.[68] In an interview with Latrobe Carroll, Cather herself explains how juxtaposition works:

> What I always want to do is make the "writing" count for less and less and the people for more. In this new novel [My Ántonia] I'm trying to cut out all analysis, observation, description, even the picture-making quality, in order to make things and people tell their own story simply by juxtaposition, without any persuasion or explanation on my part.
>
> Just as if I put here on the table a green vase and beside it a yellow orange. Now those two things affect each other. Side by side they produce a reaction which neither of them will produce alone. Why should I try to say anything clever, or by adding colorful rhetoric detract attention from those two objects, the relation they have to each other and the effect they have upon each other? I want the reader to see the orange and the vase—beyond that, I am out of it.[69]

This concept of juxtaposition is critical to all of Cather's mastery of literary technique. Because juxtaposition involves the relation of one detail to another, each detail is significant and must be placed with utmost care. Because the meaning of two details is found in their relationship, in the reaction they produce by existing side by side, the artist can write with the utmost compression. As Leo Stein observes:

> In a composition every element informs its neighbor. There is a kind of fusion, an interpenetration, an action at a distance, and not merely a neighborhood relation between the words of a poem or the colors of a picture. One can often show that, if a word is changed or a color altered, there is not merely a difference in meaning but that everywhere within the present field of attention there are changes which are utterly incapable of analysis.[70]

Cather understood this principle long before Stein, and she approached her writing confident that each word, each detail, could and should contribute to an artistic whole; she knew that inappropriate words and unnecessary details demeaned the art of literature. Cather's facility in handling both the selection and arrangement of detail is so highly developed that the resulting prose is elegant and seemingly effortless, and the composition often defies analysis. Linda Pannill says, "At its best the result is smooth perfection that sends us skidding across the surfaces without finding a rift or a snag in which to gain a foothold."[71] We must, therefore, look at the works in terms of their details, their relation to one another, and their final effect on the reader.

As we have seen, Cather bridges a gap between nineteenth-century naturalism and twentieth-century modernism, not because she practiced both, but because she identifies the processes by which each operates. She offers a corrective to the overblown novel as she found it; "too much detail is apt, like any other form of extravagance to become slightly vulgar."[72] With this observation, Cather points the way to the modern and minimalist concept of art. We see that the need to explore new limitations within which to work is as pressing a need for Cather as the need to set those limitations. As she found new forms and structures for the expression of the things that teased her mind, she worked out a series of experiments that rightly belong in the modern canon. Cather achieved such skill in handling her material and developing her own techniques, however, that their innovative nature and importance in her work have not been acknowledged, so successfully did she integrate them into that stylistic beauty and clarity of expression for which she has been recognized. Cather's view of the world in which she lived was, like Proust's, "bifocal"; that is, she had the ability to see the present in terms of the past with no middle ground to diminish the effect of one on the other. With this outlook, Cather anticipated the modernist sensibility. But, perhaps most important, she emphasizes the emotional effect of juxtaposition within the text on the reader.

Peter Faulkner identifies one of the characteristics of modernism as an interest in the result of the creative process, the work of art and its creation, rather than in the mind of the artist, the creative force beyond the made thing. Thus, the reader, viewer, or listener relates to the work of art and not to the artist; the success of a work of art, as Cather always maintained, depends on the response that the work can elicit in its audience. As Peter Faulkner says, this understanding "gives an important insight into the way that modernist poems and novels often work, their structure expressing an emotion rather than putting forth an argument."[73] With her example of the vase and the orange, Cather illustrates that the relationship in the juncture of those two ob-

jects as they appear to the reader takes form in the minute gap
that occurs between perception of one and then the other.[74] To
discuss both Cather's technique and her ability to elicit an emotional response from the reader, we need a critical vocabulary
that addresses the problem of the gap between the elements of
juxtaposition. Before we can deal with Cather's reader, we must
deal with a technique that she developed through the use of juxtaposition: the use of the gap that results from juxtaposition.

3

Fiction's Vacuoles: Tracing What
Willa Cather Left Out

As chapter 2 demonstrates, Willa Cather's technique involves the effects of juxtaposition and the gaps that it produces. Because Cather sees a work of art as a whole, we are well advised to regard the details and the gaps of juxtaposition also as part of the whole. In a comment about Willa Cather's method of writing, Edith Lewis provides a clue to an understanding of the importance of this artistic technique:

> In writing the story, it was the flooding force of a great wealth of impressions that she had to control. She could have written two or three *Sapphiras* out of her material; and in fact she did write, in her first draft, twice as much as she used. She always said it was what she left out that counted.[1]

In the juxtaposition of two seemingly unrelated episodes, scenes, events, or details, the reader will experience an intense moment of realization, drawing on or based in both elements, but occurring in neither. Perhaps the most intriguing and perplexing aspect of Willa Cather's work is the effect on the reader of what he or she cannot find on the written page. "What was left out" is significant in a special way for Cather; in fact, Miss Lewis also writes that "occasionally she outlined beforehand her plan for a novel; but she always left out its real theme, the secret treasure at its heart, the thing that gave it its reason for being."[2] What was left out must therefore be significant for the reader, because it is in that void that we find the real meaning of her work. We also begin to suspect that we are being manipulated by the artist's use of this technique in such a way that we cooperate in the story that appears in print and the story that exists in the blank spaces. Indeed, we have no choice but to participate in what Emerson calls "creative reading."

Dealing with a writer who places so much importance on what she leaves out—and who tells us so—can be exasperating because it is difficult to explicate the ephemeral. Cather herself tries to identify what, for her, is the essence of creation:

> Whatever is felt upon the page without being specifically there—that, one might say, is created. It is the inexplicable presence of the thing not named, of the overtone divined by the ear but not heard by it, the verbal mood, the emotional aura of the fact or the thing or the deed, that gives high quality to the novel or the drama, as well as to poetry itself.[3]

Here she uses metaphor, a poet's tool, in an attempt to explain the "inexplicable," but the metaphors she uses still leave us unsatisfied, with no appreciation of the concrete effect she actually has on the consciousness of her reader. In his preface to On Writing, Stephen Tennant calls Cather's vision "a poet's vision, simplified by an extraordinary natural honesty and warmth";[4] however, when he discusses "Willa Cather's preoccupation as an artist—the bringing into being of something beyond the situation or character of a story, something beyond the story itself, the unseen vision, the unheard echo, which attend all experience,"[5] his only extension of Cather's own metaphor is the image of "the room beyond," which minimally enlarges our understanding.

In any discussion of Willa Cather's style, we must try to describe in the available vague language real gaps in both the content and form of her fiction. Given her own statements about the importance of these gaps, we are compelled to keep looking for a point of entry. Some critics note her increasing use of this technique in her later books, in which it does become pronounced, unfavorably. For instance, Granville Hicks uses the phrase "highly episodic" in his discussion of Death Comes for the Archbishop,[6] and Lionel Trilling refers to her essay, "The Novel Démeublé," as "the rationale of a method which Miss Cather had partly anticipated in her earlier works and which she fully developed a decade later in Shadows on the Rock." He continues with a comment that illustrates not only the inadequacy of language to pinpoint the technique but also his own inadequacy to understand it: "And it is no less obvious that this technical method is not merely a literary manner but the expression of a point of view toward which Miss Cather had always been moving—with results that, to many of her readers, can only indicate the subtle failure of her admirable talent."[7]

Others feel the power and simplicity that Cather attains through this puzzling technique and try various ways of defining it. Rebecca West calls it "that feat of making a composition out of the different states of being";[8] E. K. Brown says, "Her vision is of essences. . . . [S]he could disengage her essential subject and make it tell upon the reader with a greater directness and power, help it to remain uncluttered in his mind."[9] In *Willa Cather's Imagination*, David Stouck discusses *Death Comes for the Archbishop* as a book that

> moves, then, not in familiar chronological sequence but through the juxtaposition of episodes and narratives which are loosely associated with the ideal of saintliness, and which offer an edifying or emotional contrast to each other. . . . Any action in the novel is almost always described "after the event"; what is important is not the event, but the effect.[10]

The effect, as we have seen, is all-important, and these critics are perceptive enough to appreciate any technique that can achieve that effect. They all deal with the events of the story as given, however; they do not address themselves to the gaps between the events and to the functions those gaps perform, because they do not have the critical vocabulary to do so.

Edward and Lillian Bloom do address this problem of critical vocabulary directly in their book, *Willa Cather's Gift of Sympathy*. They point out Cather's own inability to define clearly her technique, and they suggest that it was necessary for her "to fall back upon a language of subjective response." They continue:

> This haziness—if such it may be called—was unavoidable, for she was reflecting rather than asserting, and her subject matter was of such private intensity that it simply did not lend itself to a critical rationale. . . . Terms such as "desire," "yearning," and "spirit" may seem elusive when attempts are made to compress them into these definitions. They are abundantly clear in narrative context, however, generally eliciting the response of feeling when incisive statement is inadequate.[11]

Incisive statement is inadequate because, thus far, we have been unable to address the problem of "what was left out." Our discussions have considered what was included; now we must begin to confront the voids that shape these modern texts and give us the space in which to experience an astonishing, emotional "reader response." Once we can name the unnamed, we can begin to see how Cather uses it.

I would like to propose that we borrow a term used in science, a biologic or botanical metaphor, to name this elusive technique. We can call the unwritten but essential part of Willa Cather's fiction, the *vacuole*. I suggest this term because it functions in the same way for science that we need it to function in our understanding of Willa Cather, and because it fills our need for an identifying critical term with which to address the artistic technique Cather employs. It is far more manageable than the unwieldy terminology of current reader-response analysis: *lacunae of indeterminacy, blanks, negations,* or *indeterminate areas in imagination;* it recognizes the structural significance of the technique as well as its referentiality better than the term *allusion;* and it is more precise than *gap,* because it carries with it the weight of its scientific meaning as well.

There occur in nature, specifically in cells themselves, empty spaces which scientists have named *vacuoles.* Although they are now discovering that some vacuoles are not actually empty— just as the gaps between the details in juxtaposition are not really empty once the reader has perceived their significance—biologists and botanists as well as physicians and physiologists still use the term for both animal and plant cell definition. In both kinds of cell, the vacuole helps to maintain the structure of the cell. In animal cells, the vacuole often performs functions such as storage, ingestion, digestion, excretion, and expulsion of excess water; plant cell vacuoles also "serve to expand the plant cell without diluting its cytoplasm,"[12] thus enabling the plants themselves to attain a large size without accumulating the bulk that would make metabolism difficult. In "Problems in Water Relations of Plants and Cells," Paul J. Kramer explains that

> we are concerned with vacuoles as osmotic systems that develop the turgor pressure essential for mechanical support of unlilgnified tissues, for certain movements of plant structures such as the leaves of sensitive plants, for opening of stomata and for cell expansion. Loss of turgor pressure as a result of dehydration causes cessation of growth and wilting.[13]

In other words, both plant and animal vacuoles appear empty, though neither actually is empty; both are supported by, and in turn support, the structure of the cell; plant vacuoles, in fact, allow the plant to develop a structure that is greater in size than would logically, or scientifically, be expected.

In addition to these specific meanings of vacuole, scientists are apt to use the word in a more general sense to refer to any unusual empty space in the natural order. For instance, to a geologist, a fluid inclusion in a mineral is a vacuole. In his definition of vacuole, which refers only to cytology, Joseph G. Hoffman notes the wide variety of those phenomena called vacuoles, pointing out that "they come and go and vary widely in size."[14] Thus, the term is vested with a wide range of applications for its use in understanding Willa Cather's literary technique, referring to gaps in plot sequence, which any reader may notice, and also to those absences resulting from Cather's selection of detail, which only a reader familiar with the history of her composition would know with equal significance. Its usefulness derives from its potential to identify structural absences that, in fact, allow for a fuller story than should be technically possible; the excisions themselves vary widely in size. The beauty of the term is its adaptability to the text at hand.

In science, as in art, language reverberates with many layers of meaning and association. I. A. Richards points out that "a metaphor may be illustrative or diagrammatical, providing a concrete instance of a relation which would otherwise have to be stated in abstract terms. This is the most common scientific or prose use of metaphor."[15] It is interesting to note that the scientist is as particular as the poet about the connotative power of the word. In the interest of clarification and specificity, S. M. McGee-Russell proposes a further refinement of vacuole: "it is now desirable to have some special terminology to describe them and set them apart from other organelles. For an empty-seeming vacuole I suggest the term colamphora."[16] The term McGee-Russell suggests is the name of an ancient Greek, two-handled water vessel. We are reminded of Owen Barfield's conclusion: "How essentially parochial is the fashionable distinction between Poetry and Science as modes of expression."[17] We must agree, therefore, that the vacuole serves as a metaphor in the scientific or prose sense: it represents an abstract relation in a concrete term.

Richards reminds us, however, that "metaphor had yet further uses. It is the supreme agent by which disparate and hitherto unconnected things are brought together in poetry for the sake of their effects upon attitude and impulse which spring from their collocation and from the combination which the mind then establishes between them."[18] For vacuole to work poetically, it must be the catalytic agent for the imagination. Willa Cather once told Elizabeth Sergeant that she could only describe this coming together of the two elements of the book [*O Pioneers!*] as a sudden inner explosion and enlightenment. She had experienced it before only in the conception of a poem. Now she would hope always for similar experience in creating a novel, for the explosion seemed to bring with it the inevitable shape that is not plotted but designs itself. She now believed that the least possible tinkering with the form—revealed from within—the better.[19]

Emily Dickinson said that this same explosion took the top of her head off;[20] Barfield more sedately describes this experience as a "felt change of consciousness," the goal of the "aesthetic imagination," and he explains, "'consciousness' embraces all my awareness of my surroundings at any given moment, and 'surroundings' includes my own feelings. By 'felt' I mean to signify that the change itself is noticed, or attended to."[21] The explosion of understanding that Cather experienced in the coming together of the two elements of *O Pioneers!* is reflected in its form; the gap between the first two parts of the novel sets us up for an aesthetic explosion of our own. Barfield calls this "*Living* poetry . . . the present stir of aesthetic imagination lights up only when the normal continuum of this process is interrupted in such a manner that a gap is created, and an earlier impinges directly upon a later—a more living upon a more conscious."[22] This gap can be a thirteen-year space between parts of a work, or a minute space between disparate details, or an unexpected space between scenes; however, it is in this space, or vacuole, that we experience the insight arising from the juxtaposition of Cather's often disjointed elements. It is the vacuole that gives the novel its form, arising from the carefully selected material itself; it is the vacuole that sustains the structure of the work without overloading it. Among the scant details of *My Mortal Enemy* lie the unseen but swollen vacuoles of meaning in which the reader experiences the poetic change of consciousness that is the result of art.

With *O Pioneers!* Willa Cather recognized the power and rhythm she could create by the selective placement of vacuoles, and the books that follow all result from her increasing mastery of this technique, which allows her to leave out what counts. If we look closely at *Alexander's Bridge*, however, we can see the seeds of the novel *démeublé* even in this early work. As Cather becomes more and more the consummate artisan, she learns with increasing skill how to handle the elements of metaphor, the vacuole itself, and the aesthetic consciousness of her readers. It is possible to trace Cather's use of the vacuole as a technical tool throughout her work; in this study we will consider only the novels, because ample material exists for study and illustration here of both this specific technique, and her increasing experimentation with the novel's artistic form and its aesthetic effect.

In an essay called "My First Novels [There Were Two]," Cather discusses her early novels, mentioning, in fact, not only the first two books, but the first four. Her famous comparison of *Alexander's Bridge* to a studio picture is followed by an even more interesting statement:

> The impressions I tried to communicate on paper were genuine, but they were very shallow. I still find people who like that book because it follows the most conventional pattern, . . . Soon after the book was published I went for six months to Arizona and New Mexico. The longer I stayed in a country I really did care about, and among people who were a part of the country, the more unnecessary and superficial a book like *Alexander's Bridge* seemed to me. I did no writing down there, but I recovered from the conventional editorial point of view.[23]

Her use of the words *shallow, superficial,* and *conventional* is the clue to her lack of satisfaction with the book. Cather finds the vacuoles that add depth to the actual story missing here. In this work, all information is given to the reader; because appreciation of the work is a direct result of involvement in it, the reader responds in a pleasant, perhaps moving, but superficial way. It seems that Cather's problem with *Alexander's Bridge* is twofold: she is uncomfortable with its affinity to James and Wharton as well as its debt to Poe and Adams,[24] and she knows that it does not create a world beyond its pages. At one point, however, we are invited to bridge a gap. Chapter 9 ends in Bartley's apartment with our attention closely focused on Hilda and Bartley; chapter 10 begins with the long, distancing viewpoint of "a Boston lawyer who had been trying a case in Vermont."[25] By the time we have our bearings, we are back in Bartley's consciousness. This gap, though minute, triggers a subconscious reaction that all is not right. The reader's uneasiness arises from the effect of the vacuole. In her introduction to *Alexander's Bridge,* Bernice Slote notes that the work does contain many of the themes and techniques of the later novels; she also adds that "its crisply balanced form is the body carefully chosen to support the theme."[26] Even in the clearly balanced form, we can find the unsettling gap that will become the form-determining vacuole of *O Pioneers!*

We have already noted Cather's description of the writing of *O Pioneers!* as an explosion similar to the conception of a poem. She says in "My First Novels": "Here was no arranging or 'inventing'; everything was spontaneous and took its own place, right or wrong. . . . Since I wrote this book for myself, I ignored all the situations and accents that were then generally thought to be necessary."[27] By ignoring the expected situations and accents, she challenges the reader to a greater involvement in the story. Here, the superficial reading is possible, but the real— and very carefully contrived—story is not on the page. As James Woodress reminds us:

> The structure of *O Pioneers!* has troubled a good many readers. Its loose organization, gaps, and digressions have made it seem a flawed work of art. Despite Cather's insistence that the material dictated the form, and the story told itself, art is not nature, and any artist must select and arrange incident and character. Like any other novelist, Cather brings order out of chaos in creating a literary work. She gets away with loose organization, however, because plot is probably the least important part of a novel. Readers want a book to stir their emotions, stimulate their imagination; they want characters who live and breathe; images that linger in the memory after the book is closed. All of these things Cather does well.[28]

Cather is able to do all of these things well because she controls her reader's response to the events she does record. We have already mentioned earlier the thirteen-year hiatus between parts 1 and 2, which is the most obvious change in form. Here the distancing that we saw in *Alexander's Bridge* is further emphasized by a tense change from the traditional story-telling past tense to the attention-demanding present tense.

> It is sixteen years since John Bergson died. His wife now lies beside him, and the white shaft that marks their grave gleams across the wheat fields. Could he rise from beneath it, he would not know the country under which he has been asleep. The shaggy coat of the prairie, which they had lifted to make him a bed, has vanished forever.[29]

Consider the jump that the reader must make from the last sentences of part 1:

> She had never known before how much the country meant to her. The chirping of the insects in the long grass had been like the sweet-

est music. She had felt as if her heart were hiding down there, somewhere with the quail and the plover and all the little wild things that
crooned or buzzed in the sun. Under the long shaggy ridge, she felt
the future stirring. (71)

The reader is jolted here by the juxtaposition of the two images:
the future sleeping under the shaggy prairie and the Bergsons
sleeping there as well. Both point ahead to the final image of the
book, which is also foreshadowed by Alexandra's feeling that her
own heart was "hiding down there": "Fortunate country, that is
one day to receive hearts like Alexandra's into its bosom, to give
them out again in the yellow wheat, in the rustling corn, in the
shining eyes of youth!" (309). At this last point in the book, however, Cather uses the vacuole for timing and distancing; we are
put off guard, and when the insight comes, it has the effect of
an explosion because it is unexpected. By placing the accents in
the "wrong" places throughout the book, she keeps us aware of
not only the actual situations we are given, but the ones we normally anticipate in fiction.

The Song of the Lark is Willa Cather's experiment with "the
full-blooded method which told everything about everybody"
and which, she tells us, "was not natural to me."[30] In her preface
to the book, Cather observes:

> The story set out to tell of an artist's awakening and struggle; her
> floundering escape from a smug, domestic, self-satisfied provincial
> world of utter ignorance. It should have been content to do that. I
> should have disregarded conventional design and stopped where my
> first conception stopped, telling the latter part of the story by sugges-
> tion merely.[31]

Again we notice that disapproving word conventional. Both this
book and Alexander's Bridge follow someone else's rules too
closely. We should also notice, however, that Cather has enough
confidence in her own method to assert that she could tell the
latter part of the story by mere suggestion. There are gaps in
Thea's story—for instance, she never actually marries Ottenburg;
however, when Cather turns to My Ántonia, she remembers the
lesson she has learned in writing The Song of the Lark: "Too
much detail is apt, like any other form of extravagance, to become slightly vulgar; and it quite destroys in a book a very satisfying element analogous to what painters call 'composition.'"[32]

By this time, composition has come to include both the suggestive detail and the significant vacuole that attends it.

With *My Ántonia*, Cather reaches a balance between vacuole and detail that can best be considered as poetry. The image of the plough against the sun is supported by and resonates with our consciousness of all that it took to tame the prairie; the vanishing road, "like gashes torn by a grizzly's claws,"[33] recalls other roads, both those described in the book and those that we know have existed for Jim in the world beyond the novel. We can create for ourselves from the scant details the New York life Jim lives, and we can comprehend the entire relationship between Ántonia and Cuzak by reading: "Clearly, she was the impulse, and he the corrective" (358).

Jim says, "It must have been the scarcity of detail in that tawny landscape that made detail so precious" (29). In *My Ántonia* the detail is precious both because it is scarce and because it is loaded with implication. Discovering the implication, filling the vacuole, readers are drawn into the poetic creation, just as Cather intends them to be.

In a 1921 interview with Eva Mahoney for the *Omaha World-Herald*, Cather discussed her technique in writing *One of Ours* (which she originally called *Claude*):

> The hero is just a red-headed prairie boy. . . . I have cut out all descriptive work in this book—the thing I do best. I have cut out all picture making because that boy does not see pictures. It was hard to cease to do the thing that I do best, but we all have to pay the price for everything we accomplish, and because I was willing to pay so much to write about this boy I felt that I had a right to do so.[34]

Here, the vacuoles, the descriptions that are missing, are a clue to her method of characterizing Claude; what he does not see is essential to our understanding of him.

Although he does not refer to it by name, James Woodress points out one of the vacuoles in *One of Ours* that underlines the lack of "picture making" in the book. Discussing Claude's disastrous marriage to Enid, he not only locates a gap for us, he locates the source for the actual incident as well:

> On their wedding night, as the Denver Express carries them off for their honeymoon, Enid locks Claude out of their stateroom. This incident, Cather told a friend, actually happened to a young man she knew in Pittsburgh; otherwise she never would have had the courage to use it.[35]

Here, Cather transforms memory into art, employing the vacuole that real life suggests, and invites her readers to bring to the scene their own comprehension of frustration—not only the sexual frustration of the thwarted bridegroom but all the frustration of life itself.

We might consider Willa Cather's next novel, *A Lost Lady*, as entirely a characterization. Certainly it can be read as a simple story of a young man's disillusionment with an older, beautiful, and charming woman; indeed, we should note that Hollywood twice exploited the cinematic qualities of the book. Beginning with the title itself and the numerous meanings of the word *lost*, the reader brings so many conscious and unconscious associations to its details that we have several different novels arising from the same seemingly simple story. In this work, Cather uses the vacuole to swell the story beyond the limits of its structure. For instance, the spaces give us a place to reflect on the provocative names of the characters: Ivy Peters, Niel Herbert, Captain Forrester.[36] The book can be read as Mrs. Forrester's story, as Niel's story, as Captain Forrester's story; it can be read as social allegory; it can be read as a book about art itself. The number of readings one can have is determined by the number of ways in which the reader can fill the vacuoles.

Willa Cather herself called *The Professor's House* "two experiments in form." She explains:

> The first is the device often used by the early French and Spanish novelists: that of inserting the *Nouvelle* into the *Roman.* . . . But the experiment which interested me was something a little more vague, and was very much akin to the arrangement followed in sonatas in which the academic sonata form was handled somewhat freely.[37]

Her metaphor explains the three-part structure of the book and also clarifies her return in the third part to the characters and situation of the first. Her image of the turquoise set in dull silver might apply as well to our metaphor, the vacuole. In this book, it is necessary to fill the void for the reader, because most readers cannot bring Cather's experience of the Southwest to parts 1 and 3. *The Professor's House* probably demands more effort on the reader's part than any of the other works; it certainly requires several readings for the experience of the vacuole, that is, "Tom Outland's Story," to impinge on our appreciation of Godfrey St. Peter's story.

In a review of *My Mortal Enemy* entitled "Willa Cather Fumbles for Another Lost Lady," Louis Kronenberger comments unfavorably on the book's brevity:

Compression and selection grow naturally stronger in most good writers as they master their medium. But in *My Mortal Enemy* they have been carried too far. All bones and no flesh is never a wise method. In this instance Miss Cather has done ever worse—though she has used very little, she has not always used the bones. Significant things are left out, and the reader is left not only unsatisfied, but also puzzled.[38]

Certainly this short work makes every detail count: both placement and timing of the vacuoles draw the reader into the story in such a way that reading it can be an exhausting experience. Vacuoles are used here as gaps in the plot, as signals to both emotional changes and to narrative voice changes, and as the keys to an entire structure of relevance beyond the page. For instance, Nellie says at one point:

> For many years I associated Mrs. Henshawe with that music, thought of that aria as being mysteriously related to something in her nature that one rarely saw, but nearly always felt; a compelling, passionate, overmastering something for which I had no name, but which was audible, visible in the air that night, as she sat crouching in the shadow. When I wanted to recall powerfully that hidden richness in her, I had only to close my eyes and sing to myself: "*Casta diva, casta diva!*"[39]

In *Music in Willa Cather's Fiction*, Richard Giannone discusses the aria, which, as Cather tells us in the novel, comes from the opera *Norma*.[40] He elucidates this reference fully, explaining the resemblances between Myra and Norma. It is also fascinating to discover that the next line after the aria is "mira, Norma, mira." What makes this a vacuole and not merely a literary allusion is the very real amplification of Myra's character that the whole of the opera *Norma* provides. Every detail and reference in the book can in some fashion be expanded in just this way. If this is the case, then we can experience in *My Mortal Enemy* a novel with the breadth and density of *The Song of the Lark*.

We have mentioned the critical dismay at the episodic nature of *Death Comes for the Archbishop*; even those who praise its mood have some difficulty classifying this work as a novel. Because Cather intends to arouse the aesthetic imagination of her reader, she supplies both fact and vacuole; the emotional and psychological impact of this beautifully written novel comes in part from the reader's own consciousness of the process of creation. The scene with the Bishop of Durango, in which Father Latour secures the letters containing his credentials and establishing his authority, takes place only in our imagination, but it is as real as if Cather had described it and is perhaps more significant than if it had actually appeared on the page. We have such a vivid impression of Father Vaillant that we undertand without any explanation the characteristics of his own bishopric in Colorado. This book is extraordinary because we are not particularly aware that the conventional main events are missing; it is only when we search for some specific bit of information that we *should* be able to locate that we realize we have absorbed it in the gaps, we have been manipulated through the vacuoles. We are less aware of our own efforts in this book than in any other; we are only cognizant of that "felt change" in our consciousness and understanding of human relations.

Marion Marsh Brown and Ruth Crone call *Shadows on the Rock* "a long lyric prose poem, sincere, genuine and charming,"[41] and John Randall agrees with their assessment of the book:

> All of Willa Cather's novels can be considered to be extended lyrics in prose; on this basis *Shadows on the Rock* is better constructed than the previous novel because in it the unity of lyric tone is consistently maintained.[42]

Cather creates this tone through the small, homey, familiar details she uses in presenting this fairly circumscribed world of seventeenth-century Quebec. By juxtaposing the serenity of the town with glimpses of the wilderness that surrounds it, however, Cather creates a vacuole in which we instinctively know how much this serenity costs. When we read the novel, the vacuoles give us space for reflection; the gap between Cécile's understanding of Mother Catherine de Saint-Augustin and Mother Juschereau's view of her allows us to reflect on the gap between civilized France and civilized Quebec more efficiently than any description could. This example demonstrates Catherian compression at its best. The vacuoles in *Shadows on the Rock* account for the intentionally nostalgic air about the book; the leisurely movement of the story is controlled by their placement. David Stouck says:

> The painterly quality for which Willa Cather's style is distinguished is strongly developed here; each chapter in the novel constitutes a self-controlled, essentially plastic scene and almost every sequence

of the book is set in a descriptive tableau which superbly evokes the colors and textures of the Quebec landscape.[43]

When we first approach Lucy Gayheart, it appears to be, as Maxwell Geismar says, "a standard and almost stereotyped story in our literature; the love affair of the young provincial girl who seeks an artistic career and the sophisticated city-man who represents all the glamour of artistic success." He continues in admiration of the technique that can persuade readers to forget what they see:

> what Cather had managed to create in the reader of her story is hardly so much that "willing suspension of disbelief" which the literary critic delights in, but a sort of inevitable and unwitting acceptance of the artist's intention—an intention that is hardly limited to a picture of love's delights.[44]

We have seen that Cather intentionally enlists the reader's participation in the creation of her work; "unwitting" or aware, we are forced by the inevitable effect of the work's structure to accept her premises. In this particular novel, vacuoles are left between each of the books, but they follow scenes of such emotional intensity that we rush into the void propelled by our own momentum. We feel Lucy's anguish at Sebastian's death more deeply because we do not see it. We respond to Harry Gordon's remorse and guilt with his own helplessness because we bridge the twenty-five years he has endured it in the time it takes to turn the page; the horror is fresh to us—we have just perceived it—in the same way that it remains fresh to Harry after all those intervening years.

In this work, Cather also uses the vacuole as a void that invites the reader to enrich the story through association. References to specific works of music are significant in this novel, as they are in both The Song of the Lark, and My Mortal Enemy; in Lucy Gayheart, we find references to some of Cather's other novels. The Chicago Art Institute appears here with its promise of the immortality of art for Lucy as well as for Thea in The Song of the Lark; drowning is the cause of death for Bartley Alexander, Sebastian, and, finally, Lucy.[45] Both of the earlier works elucidate and amplify the events and themes of Lucy Gayheart.

Edith Lewis calls Sapphira and the Slave Girl "uncharacteristic," in the sense that one does not find in it the qualities one most looks to find; the qualities that most predominate in the writer's other work. But this, perhaps, comes not so much from a lack, as from an emergence, a substitution of other latent traits in the writer's development. It is written austerely, with very little of that warmth and generous expansion so many of her readers delight in. . . . Nothing is stressed—incidents, scenes are touched on so lightly, one is hardly aware of their having more than a surface significance. Yet one finds—I find, at least—that they have a curiously imperishable quality.[46]

The quality that Lewis calls curious can be attributed to Cather's childlike world view, which Pers described. In this novel Cather tests the imaginative ability of the child's vision and her reader's ability to participate in that vision. Lewis's point that one is scarcely aware of what is significant is a tribute to Cather's crafted contrivance of the vacuoles supporting the work. The various digressions within the book are such a part of the apparently seamless whole that the reader's response to them is almost unconscious. As Susan Rosowski points out, however, "the overall effect of these disruptions is that this novel, which seems to offer a retreat into the past, contains the distinctly modern search for meaning in an estranged world."[47]

Sapphira and the Slave Girl gives us ambiguities and the space in which to experience them; by the end of the novel, we are as ambiguous about Sapphira as her husband, daughter, and Nancy's mother Till. The final chapter, which takes place twenty-five years after the rest of the book and includes the child Willa as a character, threatens to become a Cather "convention," an epilogue following a vacuole of compressed time. Here, though, the central action of this last part is related by Till and sends us back in time; we are forced to cross the gap both coming and going. Even in this late book, Cather remains in charge of her material, her technique, and her reader.

Willa Cather manipulates the few details of her work to produce the greatest emotional impact on her reader in a deliberate way. We have also noted the many ways in which she uses the void, or the vacuole, to achieve many of her artistic goals. Implicit in this theory of reader manipulation is a theory of reader response. We shall see in chapter 4 that Willa Cather not only anticipates the modern attitude toward juxtaposition and experimentation in technique, but she also anticipates the integral role of the reader in the creative process of modern literature.

4

Willa Cather and the "Fine Reader":
Art as a Mutual Endeavor

In *Willa Cather's Gift of Sympathy*, Edward and Lillian Bloom make an important statement regarding Willa Cather's relation to her readers. They say:

> Miss Cather, it seems to us, invited the sympathy of her readers to both her fiction and her critical explanations. She took for granted a measure of kindred feeling, assuming that in the absence of a perhaps intuitive understanding of her aims no definition or objective enlargement could instill the emotions which she portrayed and hoped to share. . . . Terms such as "desire," "yearning," and "spirit" may seem elusive when attempts are made to compress them into these definitions. They are abundantly clear in narrative context, however, generally eliciting the response of feeling when incisive statement is inadequate.[1]

As we have seen earlier, Cather believes that the writer's greatest gift is sympathy with his or her material, by which she means the ability of the writer to give himself over to the material. We also find that Cather expects that same kind of sympathy from her readers for her created work. Through the work, the writer and reader are joined in a mutual experience that depends on a shared emotional response to the created text. Bernice Slote points out that "'feel' is Willa Cather's shorthand for the living experience of art" and stresses Cather's opinion:

> As a pinprick can separate the living from the dead, so feeling is the simplest evidence of some reality created through the imagination. The absolute necessity in art is the personal encounter. The artist or the work succeeds if the thing works—if there is a response.[2]

The concept of reader response, codified in the 1970s as a phenomenological approach to literature by such authorities as Roman Ingarden, Wolfgang Iser, and Horst Ruternof, is also found in the theories, expectations, and artistic practices of Willa Cather, though she necessarily looks at the reader from a different viewpoint. In this chapter, we will examine Cather's concept of the sensitive reader, the role of the reader and the responsibility of the writer to that reader, and the critical importance of the techniques used in the manipulation of the reader to produce that essential emotional response to the work of art.

Cather's affinity with the modernists is never clearer than when we consider her attitude toward the reader. David Craig observes that "we can see that a main effort of Modernism was to set a gulf between the 'quality' and the popular."[3] In the 1924 *Times* interview with Rose Feld, Cather expresses her distinction between earlier work produced for a reading public and that enjoyed by the "cinema" public. In a statement that certainly gives truth to a certain disenchantment with the present attitude toward art, she says: "It's the same thing that is responsible for the success of the cinema. It is . . . a cinema public for whom this reading material is published. . . . This public [cultivated people] doesn't exist today any more than the cinema public existed then."[4] Ezra Pound puts the issue succinctly: "The art of popular success lies simply in never putting more on any page than the most ordinary reader can lick off in his normally rapid half-attentive skim-over."[5] We should note, however, that Willa Cather does not completely denigrate this sort of popular writing nor this cinema audience; she is merely exercising that ability of hers to set limits. Amusement is perfectly acceptable in its place; however, it has nothing to do with art.[6] In "The Novel Démeublé," she says: "In any discussion of the novel, one must make it clear whether one is talking about the novel as a form of amusement, or as a form of art; since they serve very different purposes and in very different ways."[7] The reader for whom Cather writes, and who deserves the designation "fine reader," can also distinguish between "quality" and "popular." She defines what she means by a "fine reader" in the same interview with Feld:

> I mean the person with quickness and richness of mentality, fineness of spirituality. . . . It's the shape of the head that's of importance, the something in it that can bring an ardor and honesty to a masterpiece and make it all over until it becomes a personal possession.[8]

For such a reader, the act of reading is itself a creative enterprise:

the reader must have a sympathetic relation with the subject-matter and a sensitive ear; especially must he have a sense of "pitch" in writing. He must recognize when the quality of feeling comes inevitably out of the theme itself; when the language, the stresses, the very structure of the sentences are imposed upon the writer by the special mood of the piece.[9]

Cather describes the relationship between writer and reader as resembling the relationship between friends. She maintains:

We like a writer much as we like individuals; for what he is, simply, underneath his accomplishments. Oftener than we realize, it is for some moral quality, some ideal which he himself cherishes, though it may be little discernible in his behavior in the world. It is the light behind his books and it is the living quality in his sentences.[10]

In this description we notice some of the vague critical language that the Blooms identify. We can also appreciate the ability that Cather has of communicating exactly what she means in textual context.

In her introduction to Peter Ackroyd's *Notes for a New Culture*, Anne Smith proposes that a major hindrance to a creative criticism in the twentieth century has been the failure of the critic to learn from the artist. She says: "Very few can be seen to have taken to heart that most important dictum of the modern, 'I write: let the reader learn to read.'"[11] Cather's reader must learn to read the text for what is recorded and for what is left unsaid. We can better learn to understand Cather's techniques if we consider them in terms of her relationship with the reader.

Very much of what Willa Cather has done to literature has been done in an attempt to communicate an emotional experience from writer to reader, from one sensitive creating imagination to another sensitive receptive one. Ellmann and Feidelson discuss this as a trend of modern literature, observing that

modern literature has elevated individual existence over social man, unconscious feeling over self-conscious perception, passion and will over intellection and systemic morals, dynamic vision over the static image, dense actuality over practical reality.[12]

Certainly we can agree that Cather would approve of each of these distinctions, arguing that the felt connections are the important ones, that passion is essential to art, and that reality is best suggested rather than described. Cather's sensitive reader is equipped to cooperate with her in realizing the "dense actuality" of her novels.

By making the distinction between "quality" and "popular" writing, the modern writer demonstrates a respect for the serious reader. As Frank Lentricchia points out, we have discovered that "reading is not carried on by a transparent neutral self, but is a form of creation and a will to mastery."[13] This respect for the reader is evident in Cather's attitude toward the audience whom she regards as her "friends," and with whom she intends to share her own experience in the form of art. As Jean Lavon Throckmorton notes:

> From the point of view of the appreciator (in Willa Cather's case, of course, the reader) art was to be another life experience. . . . It is perhaps simplest, if not most poetic, to say that Willa Cather had had intense emotional experiences, and her art was intended to give these to her readers.[14]

When Cather proposes in "On the Art of Fiction" that the whole of the artistic process should be simplification "so that all that one has suppressed and cut away is there to the reader's consciousness as much as if it were in type on the page,"[15] she establishes the mutual responsibility of reader and writer in the creation of art: the writer must use language so carefully and choose detail so specifically that the reader will respond in the expected manner. The reader must bring to the work of art an openness to suggestion, an appreciation of the subject matter, and a capacity for feeling.

Perhaps the clearest explanation of what Cather expected from both storyteller and reader is found in Shadows on the Rock when Mother Juschereau relates the story of Mother Catherine de Saint-Augustin to Cécile. George Greene uses this example to illustrate the point in his article, "Willa Cather's Grand Manan":

> After listening, rapt, while a kind nun concludes a story woven to lead from suspense to self-confrontation, Cécile cuts short Mother Juschereau's zeal to add a moral. "N'expliquez pas, chere Mere, je vous en supplie!" . . . The storyteller has done her work. Now the hearer has both the right and the duty to weigh implications. That one scene encapsulated Willa Cather's mature approach to narrative.[16]

We can find this same attitude expressed in various ways by

several of Cather's literary successors. Arthur Koestler says: "The artist objectifies some aspects of his experience in the creation of a character, and the reader re-creates the character out of *his* own experience, using the text as a catalyzing agent."[17] George Szanto suggests that the reader must make a "leap from external reality to the immediacy of the poem"[18] for this new kind of writing to be successful. Robert Crosman challenges the old belief that writers alone make meaning when he argues, "Yes, authors do make meaning (since we go on insisting that they must) but— many of us are finding it increasingly necessary to say—yes, readers make meaning."[19] For Cather, a piece of writing is successful only if the reader has shared the writer's vision and internalized the emotion that it expresses. She says:

> One might say that every fine story must leave in the mind of the sensitive reader an intangible residue of pleasure; a cadence, a quality of voice that is exclusively the writer's own, individual, unique. A quality which one can remember without the volume at hand, can experience over and over again in the mind but can never absolutely define, as one can experience in memory a melody, or the summer perfume of a garden.[20]

We should recall Cather's notion that a reader likes a writer as one likes any individual, and we should also remember that for Cather style is "a way of seeing and feeling things, a favourite mood."[21] We can therefore expand our notion that style is a way of organizing one's interests, expressed in techniques that demonstrate those interests, to include the role of the reader, the receiver, on whom the effects of this unique style must tell. Style is defined to some extent by the success of its effects on the reader. In *Willa Cather, The Paradox of Success*, Leon Edel comments, "Literary art, it seems to me, is the most personal creation of man: it is the use of words to express feeling and experience in story and poem, in metaphor and simile."[22] For all the impersonality of Willa Cather's public image, her relationship with her reader through the text is highly personal.

Given her notion that readers must become emotionally involved with the text, that they must make the writer's experience their own, easily recalled through suggestion, we must recognize that Cather anticipated the critics who have recently begun to study just what happens when a reader reads a text.[23] Intrinsic to this approach to literature is the question of reader manipulation. Cather has told us that art should simplify so that all that has been cut away is present to the reader's consciousness. As James Woodress has observed, "The trick was to make the reader's consciousness supply the material suppressed and cut away."[24]

Robert Scholes and Robert Kellogg discuss the bond between writer and reader in their essay "The Problem of Reality: Illustration and Representation." They say:

> Meaning, in a work of narrative art, is a function of the relationship between two worlds: the fictional world created by the author and the "real" world, the apprehendable universe. When we say we "understand" a narrative, we mean that we have found a satisfactory relationship or set of relationships between these two worlds. In some narratives the author tries to control the reader's response more fully than in others.[25]

I would like to suggest that Willa Cather consciously controls the response of her reader by several techniques. First, we shall see that she draws on the common intellectual background that she assumes to exist between herself and her reader. Second, she experiments with narrative point of view in order to involve the reader most completely in the story. Third, she incorporates cinemagraphic techniques, which increase the probability that the reader will "see" as she does.[26] Finally, she uses juxtaposition—by which I mean the side-by-side placement of any two elements of her work and the vacuole between them—to produce in her readers that felt change of consciousness, which is the hallmark of real art.

In her essay "Joseph and His Brothers," Cather points out that "the Book of Genesis lies like a faded tapestry deep in the consciousness of almost every individual who is more than forty years of age."[27] By drawing on this "tapestry" deep in her reader's consciousness, Cather can elicit a variety of responses. On the one hand, she can draw from her readers a response of recognition. The garden theme in *My Ántonia*, with its emphasis on salvation, is reinforced by a familiarity with the garden stories in the Old and New Testaments. On the other hand, she can set up a situation in which our expectations are reversed, in which the codes that we expect to hold true are turned around on us. In this instance, we might look to *One of Ours* for an example of the garden theme reversed, for, as Claude plants and beautifies his home, it becomes a symbol of sterility rather than a place of abundance and fruitfulness. The use of symbols and allusions is not unique to Cather, or even to modern writers. Cather's use of symbol, image, and allusion is interesting because of both the wide range of reference she employs and the often unexpected response she evokes. Jonathan Raban tells us that "a system of symbolism usually depends on the existence of a commonly known body of ideas or beliefs. In Western literature three basic systems recur most frequently: the symbolism of Christianity, of classical mythology, and of Romanticism."[28] Cather could add to these three systems a deep understanding of both the Southern tradition and the pioneer attitude, each of which has its own symbols and codes. The use to which she put this wide, deep, symbol-making body of ideas was not merely to set up symbol systems in her books. It is true that much of the imagery is symbolic—the most striking example would perhaps be the plough against the sun in *My Ántonia*—but much of the unwritten overtone of the books comes from the reader's intuitive understanding of any one of these systems. The manipulative potential of this common understanding arises from the contrast between the reader's expectations and whether or not Cather meets or upends those expectations.[29] In *Science and Human Values*, J. Bronowski explains how this kind of reader involvement leads to a certain mutuality of creation. He says:

> I found the act of creation to lie in the discovery of a hidden likeness. The act of creation is therefore original; but it does not stop with its originator. The work of art or of science is universal because each of us re-creates it.
>   We are moved by the poem, we follow the theorem, because in them we discover again and seize the likeness which their creator first seized. The act of appreciation re-enacts the act of creation, and we are (each of us) actors, we are interpreters of it.[30]

Cather's perception is much the same and she readily admits to drawing on the old stories that can be discovered by the reader. Indeed, she says, "This is one of the advantages of making a new story out of an old one which is a very part of the readers' consciousness. The course of destiny is already known and fixed for us, it is not some story-teller's make-believe."[31] When a writer draws on such an elusive source as her reader's consciousness for a substantial degree of meaning in her work, she is putting a substantial degree of confidence in both her reader and her technique. The success of the technique can be measured only by the response that the work evokes, and response itself can be assessed only in those vague and elusive terms of which we spoke earlier. Morton Zabel is reacting to this subtle technique when he states:

No one who has read her books between 1915 and 1930 can forget their poetry of evocation and retrospective beauty—no sensitive reader can miss it today—particularly if he shared, as most Americans shared, whether intimately or by inheritance, any part of the experience that went into their making.[32]

Like many other critics, however, Zabel does not take the next step; he does not acknowledge that the reader's response has been deliberately called forth from that common inheritance by a writer skilled in her technique.

In his article "Point of View in Fiction: The Development of a Critical Concept," Norman Friedman discusses the importance of point of view to technique. Indeed, he contends that choosing a point of view is perhaps the writer's most serious decision in setting his or her artistic limits. Friedman establishes the problem of the narrator as the adequate transmission of a story to a reader, noting that the writer must determine the way information is to reach the reader, the angle and distance from which the reader will perceive the story, and who will talk to the reader. Friedman then reviews the possibilities open to the writer: omniscience, multiple selective omniscience, and selective omniscience—or third-person omniscient, third-person limited, and first-person limited point of view, depending on one's critical vocabulary. His concern with limits begins with point of view and echoes those concerns of Willa Cather, which we have mentioned earlier; Friedman's reasons for exercising choice and selectivity are also hers. As he explains:

the prime end of fiction is to produce as complete a story-illusion as possible. Given material potentially interesting, concentration and intensity, and hence vividness, are the results of working within limits, albeit self-imposed, and any lapse thereof is in all probability the result of not establishing a limiting frame to begin with or of breaking the one already established. Surely this is one of the basic principles of artistic technique in general.

Thus the choice of a point of view in the writing of fiction is at least as critical as the choice of a verse form in the composing of a poem; just as there are certain things which cannot get said in a sonnet, so each of the categories we have detailed has a probable range of functions it can perform within its limits. The question of effectiveness, therefore, is one of the suitability of a given technique for the achievement of certain kinds of effects, for each kind of story requires the establishment of a particular kind of illusion to sustain it.[33]

Although Cather once said that novels of feeling were best narrated by a character in the story and that novels of action should be told in the third person,[34] and although she kept to this principle in a general way, she actually uses a variety of different points of view throughout her work, some more experimental than others, but all suited to the individual work. The fact that she began *A Lost Lady* three times before she found the proper point of view—Niel's—indicates that she, like Friedman, considers the selection of point of view to be a critical choice. For six of the books—just half of her total output—Cather uses an omniscient narrator: *Alexander's Bridge, O Pioneers!, The Song of the Lark, Death Comes for the Archbishop,* and *Shadows on the Rock.* In two books, she lets a character tell the story: Jim is the narrator of *My Ántonia* and Nellie Birdseye, with her wonderfully appropriate name, gives the reader *My Mortal Enemy.* In both *One of Ours* and *A Lost Lady,* Cather uses the highly praised selective omniscience—or the third-person limited—technique. In *The Professor's House* and *Sapphira and the Slave Girl,* Cather uses a mixed point of view.

None of this discussion is as straightforward as the preceding list implies, and none of the books is as simple as a surface reading might suggest. Quite frequently, the voice of the omniscient narrator will change, as in *O Pioneers!,* when the narrator appears to address the reader directly, or the tone of the narrator will undergo a shift, as in *Death Comes for the Archbishop* when the scene shifts from Rome to the New (and hostile) World. In the novels in which she employs different points of view, Cather uses these as specific techniques that serve to position her reader with regard to his or her involvement in the text. She gives us Professor St. Peter's perceptions while maintaining the distance that third person produces, and she lets us hear the first-person immediacy of Tom Outland's voice, even though, in the events of the novel, he is dead. She gives us the story of Till and Nancy and Sapphira and Rachel in third-person omniscient, with the interesting exception that we do not ever know what Sapphira herself is thinking, and she lets us share the first-person excitement of the five-year-old child in the epilogue.

All of these subtle variations produce different effects on the reader and all will consequently evoke a variety of responses. For instance, Cather uses still another technique that manipulates the reader's perception of the mere facts of the story. In both *My Ántonia* and *A Lost Lady*, Cather uses framing devices that serve to make the reader doubly aware of the restricted vision of the narrative voice. David Stouck tells us that "the double perspective created by the third-person narrator,—that is, Niel's viewpoint circumscribed by an omniscient narrator—allows the reader both illusion and recognition."[35] Although the reader gets Niel's perceptions and reactions, they are filtered through a second, mediating voice—the narrator's—which may or may not be the author's. The second voice, however, makes it possible for the reader to evaluate rather than merely accept Niel's responses, and this conscious act of evaluation distances the reader from Niel. This distancing is vitally important because Marian Forrester is to be the central focus of the book; the reader cannot lose that focus by identifying too closely with Niel. Those critics who focus on Niel must acknowledge that they do so by willfully ignoring the signals Cather's point of view provides.

The frame around *My Ántonia* is supplied by the introduction attributed to the author of the book—Willa Cather. We cannot be sure that the "I" of the introduction actually does refer to Cather, however, because the work is fiction and a storyteller's domain is imagination. Here the perspective is different from that in *A Lost Lady*; no distance exists between the voice of the character Jim and the narrator because they are one. The immediacy of the events and the personal reflections of Jim are therefore just as immediate and personal to the reader. The introduction, however, sets up a third personality for the reader: the author's persona. Sharon O'Brien regards this technique as unsettling. She says:

> Does Jim speak for Cather? Or is there ironic distance between author and narrator? The answer to both questions is yes. At times Jim is Cather's mask and spokesman, whereas at times she is ironically detached from him. This wavering distance between author and narrator makes settled interpretation difficult and probably accounts for the novel's conflicting readings; it's hard to locate Cather's point of view in this text.[36]

Perhaps the reason that O'Brien finds it hard to locate Cather's point of view in the text is because it is not there. Readers respond to the author-persona point of view, to Jim's point of view, and to their own point of view regarding the story they are actively involved in creating. We might propose here that Cather uses her choice of point of view to create any number of viewpoints within the novel, none of which we can—with authority—attribute to Cather herself, and all of which are a result of her capacity to give herself over to the material in order to give back art that demands a response. One of the sources of the great emotional impact of the book is the picture-making capacity of Jim's imagination through which we experience the cycles of the book. Once again we must admire the simplicity with which Cather evokes a complex range of responses within and arising from the novel. To cite an example of the way in which the multiple viewpoint point of view technique works, we need only look at the title of the book. It has been argued that the *My* of *My Ántonia* refers to Jim, or to the "author," or to Cather herself. All can be true and probably are, for within the text itself five different characters refer to "my" Ántonia, and each of them has a right to claim her in some special way. By the time the reader has finished the book, he or she has also come to say with authority, "my" Ántonia as well.

Perhaps one of the most significant of Willa Cather's accomplishments is her experimentation with point of view. As we noted earlier, although she has not been recognized for her mastery of the masculine voice, Jim Burden, Niel Herbert, and Professor St. Peter are convincing spokesmen, and they elicit an emotional response from the reader that marks them as real, in the sense that created art is real. If we are to accept Cather's criterion of feeling as the standard for art, then we must attribute a good deal of the emotional intensity of the novels to the point of view from which we approach each one. Ellen Moers believes that "most of the passion in Willa Cather's work is in the eye of the narrator, the remembering mind, who whether male or female (it doesn't matter), is always a solitary, one of the unmated."[37] The passionate, solitary, remembering mind of a Cather narrator invites compassion and involvement from the sympathetic listening reader.

Certainly the use of point of view to restrict and manipulate the reader's perception is well developed in Cather's novels; as we have seen, she even produces multiple viewpoints within a single point of view and uses multiple points of view to produce a unified viewpoint. What makes all of this significant, however, is that she does this without any loss of that pure and clear style for which she is rightly praised. Cather's unity of style finally gives the work its integrity. In "Mixed and Uniform Prose Styles in the Novel," Leonard Lutwack observes that a uniform style is "a bond between author and reader, insuring that no different adjustment to language and viewpoint will be demanded from the reader than that established at the outset."[38] Cather demonstrates that a uniform style devised to involve the reader can, in fact, accommodate a number of variations in viewpoint and a number of shifts in point of view if the technique is carefully planned to strengthen rather than diminish that more important bond between written work and reader. Cather's primary concern is to forge a bond between her reader and his or her own version of the text rather than have her reader bonded dependently on an authoritative author who indicates some "truth" for which the struggle is less intense. Perhaps one key to the paradox of the continuing popularity of Cather's novels juxtaposed to her personally tentative and fluctuating reputation is that readers do not bond with her but with her books.

Susan J. Rosowski says that "Cather's greatness begins with this fact, with her ability to persuade us to look again at a region still generally considered flat, to see it differently."[39] René Rapin atttributes much of the force of *Death Comes for the Archbishop* to "Willa Cather's intense visualization communicated to the reader by infallible choice of the characteristic detail and extreme felicity in the selection, arrangement and economy of words."[40] Eudora Welty ponders the way in which Cather transforms the act of seeing into literature:

> All Willa Cather's prose . . . speaks of the world in such a way to show it's alive. There is a quality of animation that seems naturally come by, that seems a born part of every novel. Her own living world is around us as we read, present to us through our eyes and ears and touch. Of course, it doesn't escape us that this physical landscape is brought home to us in a way that is subjective. . . . What she has given us is, of course, not the landscape as you and I would see it, but her vision of it—a work of art.[41]

The point here that Welty does not make is that Cather actually gives us is not *her* vision but the power to create our *own* vision. This ability to make the reader "see" differently, the intense visualization of a novel, the quality of animation in her work are all a result of what we shall call Willa Cather's cinemagraphic technique. By this term we mean that Cather instinctively uses those techniques that are used in the filming of stories. Because her memories are so intensely visual, she transfers that intensity of vision into an intensity of language that reproduces for her reader the same visual impact of the original experience. To communicate those vivid impressions, she handles the elements of detail and scene much as if she were filming the story, and she expects her reader to sense this visual approach and respond to the sensual aspect of her work. The addition of the visual or sensual to the intellectual level of the novel intensifies the emotional component, and, ultimately, contributes to that integrated and satisfying whole, which is the completed work.

In an article entitled "The Author and the Motion Picture," immediately following Cather's interview with Latrobe Carroll in *Bookman*, May 1921, Benjamin B. Hampton asserts:

> Perhaps the one item that will interest *Bookman* readers is that the fame of a novelist reaches only a short distance into the social and intellectual scale. The appeal of motion pictures is to all classes, from the lowest stratum to the highest.[42]

We have noted Cather's assessment of the "cinema" public for whom her art was not intended. She certainly did not care about extending her fame much beyond the circle of readers who could appreciate what she was doing. Cather did not consider works that could appeal to such a wide range of interests as art, but she certainly must have read the article and she certainly knew what was going on in film.

It is also true that she had a disastrous relationship with the actual movie makers of Hollywood. By 1923, as James Woodress points out, Cather had achieved not only critical but also popular success:

> This made her attractive to Hollywood, and Warner Brothers managed to carry off the rights to *A Lost Lady* for a reported ten thousand dollars. The film was cast with Irene Rich as Marian Forrester and George Fawcett as the Captain. Douglass Cather, who then lived in southern California, was invited to visit the set during the filming, and the movie was premiered in Red Cloud on January 6, 1925. The local people thought the film very good, and it got favorable reviews in the press, but Cather didn't like the cinema. She said later that the picture brought her hundreds of fan letters from illiterate and sloppy people, who gave her a low opinion of movie audiences. Then in 1934 when Warner Brothers remade the film with Barbara Stanwyck, Cather was so distressed by the production that she wrote into her will an absolute prohibition against any future dramatization of her works in any form whatsoever.[43]

I would like to suggest that Cather's absolute refusal to allow any further dramatization of her work after the filming of *A Lost Lady* is rooted in her essential aesthetic doctrine. If the success of a work is dependent on the emotional response of each individual reader, then each reader creates "my" Marian, just as each reader creates "my" Ántonia. Therefore, no cinema presentation can ever be adequate, because once any character is given form, once a literary character takes on the "accidents" of any given actor or actress, the creative power of the-imagination has been eliminated from the artistic experience. As Cather said, "A movie, well done, may be very good indeed, may even appeal to what is called the artistic sense; but to the emotions, the deep feelings, never!"[44] No movie drawn from a seriously written novel or story can ever represent the reality of that created fiction, a work of art that requires cooperation between writer and reader. This is not to say, however, that a writer cannot use the same techniques in writing as film makers do in cinema to create evocative effects. We know that Willa Cather demonstrated an avid interest in all forms of art; we also know that she was open to the new and experimental. Her disenchantment with the translation of literature to cinema does not mean that she was unaffected by or insensitive to the new possibilities of film-making—that is, picture-making—technique.

Many critics have commented on the fact that the great periods of experimentation in art cross all genre and media lines. Indeed, we can demonstrate that the period immediately following World War I was particularly fruitful for all creative endeavors—art, literature, music, and film. Charles Eidsvik says, "The great periods of independent film have coincided historically and geographically with the great periods in other kinds of experimental art," and he cites the fiction forms of Joyce and Hemingway as comparable to the film experiments of Leger.[45] It is not surprising, therefore, to find that some of the techniques that we would normally associate with film will transfer quite readily to literature, if the writer has the temerity to try them. As we have seen, the modernist attitude predisposes the writer to experimentation, and Cather is no different, though less lauded, from Joyce and Hemingway in her willingness to use any technique that would produce the most effective result.[46]

In his excellent study of the development of similar techniques in differing genres, *Fiction and the Camera Eye*, Alan Speigel explores the development of James Joyce's extremely visual style in terms of the "cinematic." Interestingly, he traces Joyce's literary antecedents and discovers that the same techniques can be found in Flaubert's work. The point that he makes is one that is significant for our understanding of Cather:

> Later, I came to realize that while Joyce's visualizations were "cinematic," they were not without their literary precedents and anticipations; that they were in fact the point of culmination, as well as of transition, for a whole tradition of visualization in literature that first appeared in the formal procedures of the nineteenth-century novel; that many of the cinematic efforts to be found in Joyce's work were also to be found in Flaubert's, though Flaubert was not, of course, influenced by the cinema. Later I came to feel that Joyce, too, was not specifically influenced by the cinema. Did one really need film, then, to account for the technique of Joyce or, for that matter, of any novelist?[47]

Neither Flaubert nor Joyce nor Cather needed the cinema for influence; what they all needed and what they all had was the desire to make the reader "see." Flaubert's insistence on the value of language and the telling detail shaped the modern literary sensibility. Although Cather and Joyce took radically different approaches to style, both of them developed those techniques that we now call cinemagraphic—techniques that make the reader see—just as the great film makers used these techniques to make the viewer feel. It is not unreasonable that these concerns with audience response should produce similar techniques for eliciting it in different genres. We must recognize, however, the radical changes that this meant for a writer, who came from a long literary tradition with set patterns and conventions, compared to the film makers, who were working in a relatively new art form.

If we look for a moment at the objectives of film, we can see that these are some of the same objectives that Willa Cather set for herself in literature. Both the film maker and the writer are storytellers, and they each use their technical skills to communicate an emotional experience to an audience. Film engages the viewer's attention through surface details of events, and the film maker must find ways by which to relay the depth and fullness of the experience. Louis Giannetti notes that "film performers must act the subtext rather than the text proper,"[48] recalling Cather's "overtone divined by the ear" but not expressed on the page.

Just as the choice of point of view is perhaps the most significant choice a writer makes, the camera angle becomes such a choice for the film maker. The camera becomes the eye through which the audience sees the story. Giannetti contends that "in literature, the distinction between the narrator and the reader is clear: it's as if the reader were listening to a friend tell a story. In film, however, the viewer identifies with the lens, and thus tends to fuse with the narrator."[49] In literature such as that created by Cather and other modernists, this statement is invalid because one of their primary goals is to involve the reader in just the same way that the viewer is involved in film.

To make every word count, the writer must choose the most telling detail, the most reverberating image; so, too, will the film maker's choice of focus determine just what viewers will literally see and in what order they will perceive details. The juxtaposition of those details is planned to enlist the participation of viewers in interpretation of their meaning as they fill the vacuoles created when the camera shifts. As Eidsvik maintains, "The cinema is an audience art. Antonioni was the first hard-core modernist to understand that fact and take advantage of it."[50] Willa Cather is one of the first to understand that literature is also an audience art, and she adapted her techniques to this discovery. Perhaps Cather's sensitive readers will be found among the generation raised on film and television; David Cook states that "through hours of watching television, as children and teenagers, its members [know] the language of cinema implicitly."[51]

To identify the specifics of cinemagraphic technique, we can use Alan Spiegel's term *concretized form*, which begins as a Flaubertian technique that appears in both literature and cinema, and operates in Cather's novels. By this term he means "a way of transcribing the narrative, not as a story that is told, but as an action that is portrayed and presented, that seems to reveal itself to the reader apart from the overt mediations of the author."[52] For this technique to be successful, the story must be demonstrated at every moment; the novel must promote experience rather than reflection; and the visual impressions must be numerous, significant, and cumulative. This technique results in a "highly sensuous and visualized narrative" that is "a mode of apprehending the world, a way of seeing one's experience as determined by one's idea of experience."[53] To write in this narrative form "renders experience through scale, proportion, perspective, color and line, behavioral postures and gestures, plastic shapes and materialized actions."[54] Although it is clear that these criteria apply to the novels that she wrote, particularly to *My Ántonia, A Lost Lady, Death Comes for the Archbishop,* and *Shadows on the Rock,* Cather is not mentioned in the litany of modern writers who, according to Spiegel, developed Flaubert's concept: "We must understand the way in which novelists like Joyce, Hemingway, and Faulkner developed and refined this legacy."[55]

When Cather tells us that she wants the details and events of her work to affect each other as the orange and the green vase on a table affect each other in the perception of the observer, she is explaining the same effect that Spiegel attributes to concretized form. He says:

> Because the visual images are numerous and succeed one another on the page in a kind of unbroken visual stream, without pause for authorial comment or reflection, we tend to see the images in concretized fiction slightly faster than our minds can grasp their significance or their precise relation to one another. . . . Because of this mental delay, we also tend to see the images not only once but twice: first in their immediate visual otherness; then, by a kind of spontaneous and coordinating mental reflex, we see them again, but this time in their continuity and coherence.[56]

Here, as in Cather's theory, the writer counts for less and less, and the writing for more and more. Readers also count for more and more, because they bring to the work the coordinating and unifying consciousness. In a film, viewers must deal with details as they record them. The film maker controls the order and juxtaposition of these details to elicit some response, and we must always remember that our consciousness does not see each as an independent entity, but views these details, as Speigel and Cather both tell us, in relation to one another. Neither the orange nor the green vase is the same in juxtaposition as each is alone on the table; it is in the vacuole between them that we understand their unique relationship to one another. We must not assume, however, that by a succession of details we mean an accumulation of insignificant data that will ultimately amount to a revelation. Even for the film maker, Cather's theory of compression is essential, for viewers can keep only so many details in mind at once. The choice of detail—of focus—is even more important when one expects readers to participate in the creation of the story. Cather quotes Mérimée in "The Novel Démeublé": "L'art de choisir parmi les innombrable traits que nous offre la nature est, après tout, bien plus difficile que celui de les observer avec attention et de les rendre avec exactitude."[57] She also records her admiration of Stephen Crane's handling of detail:

> He simply knew from the beginning how to handle detail. He estimated it at its true worth—made it serve his purpose and felt no further responsibility about it. . . . If he saw one thing that engaged him in a room, he mentioned it. If he saw one thing in a landscape that thrilled him, he put it on paper, but he never tried to make a faithful report of everything else within his field of vision.[58]

In film, as in literature, the juxtaposition of one scene with another invites the viewer—or reader—to make judgments as to the significance of each. One event impinges and implicitly comments on the preceding and following ones. Nothing in Cather is without purpose; each of the inset stories or parables that perhaps appear tangential in *Sapphira and the Slave Girl* actually explicitly comments on the action of the plot.[59] The action in any film is advanced and the plot unfolded through the scene. Cather describes what she means by "scene" in "Defoe's *The Fortunate Mistress*":

> The "scene" in fiction is not a mere matter of construction, any more than it is in life. When we have a vivid experience in social intercourse, pleasant or unpleasant, it records itself in our memory in the form of a scene; and when it flashes back to us, all sorts of apparently unimportant details are flashed back with it. When a writer has a strong or revelatory experience with his characters, he unconsciously creates a scene; gets a depth of picture, and writes, as it were, in three dimensions instead of two.[60]

We notice Cather's confidence in the unconscious determination of art and her insistence on the emotional component of art; we must also note her concept of the picture-making quality of art, of the three-dimensional quality of literature. Her ability to think in these terms translates into her ability to create those intense and memorable scenes that stay then in the reader's memory to be recalled in all their power with all their seemingly unimportant details still fresh. We need only remember Emil and Marie under the mulberry tree, Ántonia resting her hand on the tree in her orchard, Thea holding a broken shard of pottery, or Lucy skating to realize the emotional intensity of the scenes from which those details come. For Cather, scene and detail are the means by which the writer engages the picture-making capacity of her readers, allowing them to personalize the experience of the story and make it part of their own memory just as it exists because it is part of Cather's memory. Perhaps the novels that best illustrate Cather's cinemagraphic techniques are *Lucy Gayheart* and *One of Ours*. Paul Comeau regards *Lucy* as "complex and experimental as anything she had written"[61] in terms of its form, and David Daiches writes:

> One remembers individual scenes rather than the shape of the novel as a whole, particularly the early scenes between Lucy and the singer, Clement Sebastian. If there is a touch of Hollywood about some of them, it can be maintained that it is good Hollywood, and good Hollywood has its place in this kind of literature.[62]

Hemingway accused Willa Cather of using bad Hollywood in *One of Ours* when he suggested that she stole the final battle scene from D. W. Griffith.[63] Frederick T. Griffiths, however, says that we see the events of the book "through Claude's eyes, and his idealism filters out, with varying success, the surrounding horror." He continues, "If the war sometimes looks like a movie, that is because Claude, like Dos Passos's Fuselli, often thinks in those terms. It was Claude, not Hemingway, who first viewed the climactic battle as the 'Big Show.'"[64] We must also point out that some of our response to Claude's version of the war comes from its deliberate juxtaposition to our own preconceived notion of war, which has been established by newsreels (and, for Cather's most recent readers, by television). When René Rapin discusses *One of Ours*, he emphasizes what we have come to appreciate as its concretized form. He says:

> The characters are little analyzed. What analysis is required when they stand revealed in dialogue and in action? Willa Cather is equally chary of description—one touch, carefully selected, is enough to make the reader see a man, an incident, a landscape. You can trust his imagination to complete the picture you suggest.[65]

Cather trusts her sensitive reader to respond to her picture-making techniques with the same sympathy that she has given to her subject and, in doing so, shares with the reader the responsibility for the creation of the realized work of art. Willa Cather once said that "art requires a vast amount of character. It's a whole lot more important than talent. It demonstrates itself in relationships the artist thinks important."[66] We might suggest that those important relationships are demonstrated in Cather's work through the principle of juxtaposition. If we consider simplicity as Willa Cather's credo, then juxtaposition must be her operating procedure.[67] As we saw in chapter 3, juxtaposition is also a central element in her manipulation of the reader's response to the text. We must recognize that her understanding of the principle of juxtaposition anticipated the theories of reader-response critics by sixty years. Cather uses this technique throughout her work, and demonstrates in that work the very operations that are described in the literary theories of Ingarden, Iser, and Ruternof. All of these theorists base their ideas on the elements of juxtaposition—two details and a gap—and the reaction of the reader to this juxtaposition. Ingarden refers to the "spots" or "places of indeterminacy" in imagination;[68] Iser talks about "blanks" and "negations";[69] and Ruternof refers to "lacunae of indeterminacy."[70] I prefer to use the metaphorically dense term vacuole, which was introduced in chapter 3 as more critically useful.

All of these terms, however, apply to the use of gaps within the text that serve to engage the reader's conscious participation in the creation of the work of art. Perhaps Iser best states the mechanics of the reader's response when he is given a vacuole-filled text:

> the text is structured in such a way that it allows for and, indeed, frequently runs counter to the given disposition of its readers. The blanks break up the connectibility of the schemata, and thus they marshal selected norms and perspective segments into a fragmented, counterfactual, contrastive or telescoped sequence, nullifying any expectation of *good continuation*. As a result, the imagination is automatically mobilized, thus increasing the constitutive activity of the reader, who cannot help but try and supply the necessary links that will bring the schemata together in an integrated gestalt. The greater number of blanks, the greater number of different images built up by the reader.[71]

Because Cather understands what will happen to readers when they are confronted by a vacuole, she is able to structure her work so that she can achieve the maximum imaginative response from those readers at the optimal point in the story. Willa Cather's technical brilliance hinges on her understanding of her readers, her respect for their imagination, and her confidence that she can manipulate that imagination. Karlheinz Stierle says:

> By exploring the possibilities of fiction, experimental literature challenges the reader to new modes of reading, thereby increasing the given repertoire of reception. The new reading procedures required by modern experimental fiction, as well as progress in the field of theory, provide us with new approaches to past fiction as well, thus enabling us to broaden our experience with literary texts.[72]

Cather has always been experimental, challenging the reader to new modes of reading and to participation in the creation of art; critical theory is now beginning to catch up with her.[73]

We shall now look closely at three of the novels, *A Lost Lady*, *The Professor's House*, and *My Mortal Enemy*, demonstrating how each illustrates the reader-involving techniques that we have discussed. Each of these books is experimental in a different way, each reflects Cather's modern sensibility, and each manifests the pellucid style and brilliant technique we recognize as Willa Cather's own.

5

A Lost Lady: Willa Cather's Tribute to James, Flaubert, and Artistic Autonomy

In his study on Willa Cather's style, David Massey observes that "although no one, including Cather, has described the démeublé style in detail, most critics concur about the novels that best manifest Cather's theory."[1] Those novels are *A Lost Lady*, *The Professor's House*, and *My Mortal Enemy*. Not only do these novels demonstrate her démeublé style, they also provide examples of the highly innovative techniques that Willa Cather developed to achieve the kind of art she considered "real," art that elicits an emotional response from the reader.

These three novels come at the midpoint of Cather's career as a novelist. They serve to demonstrate how the hypothesis we have proposed in chapters 1 to 4 can be proved through the text; they illustrate those convictions that deepened as Cather grew in artistic maturity; and they underline the fresh ways in which she experimented with each new work. We find that in these novels she works out her theories of stylistic simplicity and reader response, perfects the techniques that allow her to do so, declares her authorial debt to her literary predecessors and teachers, and establishes the artistic independence that finds full expression in *My Mortal Enemy*, the most "unfurnished" of all the works. In addition, we can appreciate in these novels Cather's extraordinary sureness in the practice of excision and, particularly in *The Professor's House*, her explorations of the uses of time and memory, both of which link her to those twentieth-century innovators called modernists.

Cather's dictum that "every fine story must leave in the mind of the sensitive reader an intangible residue of pleasure; a cadence, a quality of voice that is exclusively the writer's own, individual, unique"[2] reminds us that her ultimate concern is for the emotional effect of her work on her reader. To achieve that "staying power," which is a direct result of her manipulation of

the reader's response to the text, Willa Cather devised the techniques we have now identified to draw on her readers' common
intellectual background, to position readers in relation to the
characters and events of the story, and to bond readers to
the story itself through an intense participation in its creation.
Cather's experiments here with structure and form, point of
view, juxtaposition and its attending vacuole, complex imagery
systems, and cinemagraphic techniques affirm her skill as a consummate literary craftsman.

A Lost Lady may well have been Cather's most popular book;
as we have mentioned, it was a best seller in the 1920s. Critical
opinion has been equally favorable. Joseph Wood Krutch calls
this work "nearly perfect."[3] Granville Hicks maintains that "of
all the books between My Ántonia and Death Comes for the Archbishop, A Lost Lady is the most moving."[4] René Rapin writes:
"A Lost Lady yet deserves high praise. It is an accomplished
portrait, a masterpiece of concise narrative where every stroke
tells."[5] All of these critics judge the book in terms of conventional criteria, and each testifies to the simplicity of effect and
clarity of style that mark it as one of Cather's best. None of them,
however, points to the new kind of book that Cather has made
out of some old conventions and traditions.

A Lost Lady is structurally perfect, perhaps even more of a balanced composition than Alexander's Bridge. The book is divided
into two parts, each having nine chapters, which take place ten
years apart. The climactic scenes of each part occur in the fifth
chapter, and parallel events lead up to and away from these
scenes, which mirror each other in actual plot development and
emotional impact. This precise, symmetrical structure is not apparent, however, on a first reading of the book. Just as Willa
Cather had always said, when the form takes its shape from the
content, the skeleton, which unifies the work, is hidden in its
substance. In fact, the unobtrusive structure of this book is so
strong a unifying factor that Cather is able to make daring experiments that would otherwise disrupt what the reader-response
critics call good continuation. In this book, perhaps more than
any other, Cather is trying to create a single impression, one intense emotional reaction. That she does so by employing several
techinques that disrupt the flow of events illustrates just how
skilled she is at handling the raw material of art. Using point of
view as a means of character development, reader expectation
as a means of manipulation, and imagery as a means of cohesion,
she manages to integrate apparently disparate elements into a

satisfying whole. That her critics respond to that single "perfect" impression, without reference to those disruptive techniques, illustrates just how skilled she is at eliciting her reader's response. Susan Rosowski tells us:

> It is only after I put the book down and begin to classify, categorize, and interpret that I equate character and setting with ideas. While I am reading I am engaged on quite another level. I experience Marian Forrester; I help to create her. And in realizing this, I have come to believe that Cather's achievement in *A Lost Lady* was that she did precisely what she set out to do. She wrote about the experience of the thing and not the thing itself, the effect of Mrs. Forrester and not the character.[6]

With *A Lost Lady*, Cather rewrites her first novel in her own terms. We find evidence in this sixth book of the same influences that permeated *Alexander's Bridge* and caused her some discomfort. In this later "composition," however, Cather captures people she knows and scenes she remembers, using lessons she has assimilated from those masters James and Flaubert. In one sense, this might be read as Cather's initiation novel, in which she demonstrates that she has gone beyond her teachers, just as it has been read as Niel's initiation into the realities of life. We can see in this masterpiece what Cather meant when she said: "The thesis that no one can ever write a noble sonnet on a noble theme without repeating Wordsworth, or a mysteriously lovely lyric without repeating Shelley, is an evasion."[7] In this novel, Cather evades nothing, acknowledges her heritage, and demonstrates that she can put forth as something new, something Catherian, those lessons of her apprenticeship, recalling her own recurrent image of the Nebraska soil that will put forth new strength from pioneers like Eric Ericson, Anton Pucelik, and her own Alexandra.[8] Martin Foss says that "a creation is . . . 'new' and 'unique' not in comparison only to other objects, but with regard to its own parts or composition which have disappeared by giving way to the unconditioned simplicity of the absolute."[9] *A Lost Lady* is a reworking of the literary influences that have marked her own style; it is unique among the novels in its reference to those influences. With regard to the work as an artistic whole, its parts and composition disappear because the complex techniques Cather has developed using both detail and vacuole produce an absolute simplicity of effect.

It is commonly agreed that Cather uses Henry James's method

of indirect presentation in *A Lost Lady*. By doing so, Cather acknowledges her debt to James's lessons in literary technique. She once wrote that "his was surely the keenest mind any American devoted to the art of fiction. But it was devoted almost exclusively to the study of other and older societies than ours."[10] In this book she applies all she learned from that keen mind to the society that she knew and understood.[11] Philip Gerber explains how Cather herself refers to Niel's function as a Jamesian observing consciousness:

> Niel exists chiefly to represent the author and her attitude. Cather drafted the novel in the first person, later altering it; and, she herself explained that Niel is not a character at all, but "only a point of view," a "peephole" into the world of the Forresters, "something for Marian Forrester's charm to work on." Cather's beautiful memory of the central figure was the thing—the only thing—Willa Cather had hoped to accomplish with *A Lost Lady*—"just a delicate face laughing at you out of a miniature, no more."[12]

Not only must we notice Cather's identification of Niel as a "peephole," we must pay attention to her insistence that Marian Forrester is the central figure of the book. The difficulty that Cather had in choosing her point of view hinges on the necessity of seeing Marian from as many different angles as possible. In this book with its narrow focus, she is doing something radically different from what she did in *My Ántonia* with its broad scope and equally memorable heroine. Without the central focus of *A Lost Lady* there would be no story, for the story exists in the vacuoles that occur as Marian Forrester is juxtaposed with the other characters in relationships seen primarily from, but not limited to, Niel's perspective.

We would disagree with Gerber in his assessment of Niel's function as merely a figure to mimic Cather's own attitude. It should be obvious from her decision to rewrite the novel in the third person that the point of view is intrinsic to the final effect of the novel; if Cather had wanted only a mouthpiece, she could have used the first-person speaker to better advantage. Indeed, although Edmund Wilson suggests that she is incapable of depicting intensely emotional scenes through Niel's eyes,[13] as she demonstrated with Jim Burden in *My Ántonia*, she was certainly capable of handling the male consciousness in the first-person voice.

In this novel, Cather is concerned with creating the most complete portrait she can to elicit the greatest reader response possible. Traditionally, a consistent point of view has been considered essential for a certain unity within the novel. Modern novels have challenged this principle with great effectiveness; we need only recall Faulkner's *The Sound and the Fury* or *As I Lay Dying* to illustrate how far the novel has evolved. The framing narrator, like the one used by Cather in *My Ántonia*, does not interrupt the sequence of plot in the same way that a change of point of view does. Citing Percy Lubbock's *The Craft of Fiction*, Norman Friedman discusses the way in which the third-person point of view allows continuity of reader involvement with a character:

> One of the chief means to this end, the one that James himself not only announced in theory but followed in practice, is to have the story told as if by a character in the story, but told in the third person. In this way the reader perceives the action as it filters through the consciousness of one of the characters involved, yet perceives it *directly* as it impinges upon that consciousness, thus avoiding that removal to a distance necessitated by retrospective first person narration: "the difference is that instead of receiving his report we now see him in the act of judging and reflecting; his consciousness, no longer a matter of hearsay, a matter for which we must take his word, is now before us in the original agitation" (Lubbock).[14]

To judge the accuracy of this statement, we have only to recall that intensely agitating moment outside Mrs. Forrester's bedroom windows, and Niel's headlong rush away from reality: "In that instant between stooping to the windowsill and rising, he had lost one of the most beautiful things in his life."[15] Cather demonstrates her mastery of the limited third person in every scene perceived through Niel's consciousness. His is the consistently romantic and idealistic view of life and its participants, remarkably unshakable when confronted with disillusioning reality and surprisingly renewed again and again when faced with Marian Forrester's charm. At the end of the novel, his attitude toward her—or toward what she has come to represent for him—remains fascinated and protective: "'So we may feel sure that she was well cared for, to the very end,' said Niel. 'Thank God for that!'" (174).

George Szanto explains that "if the narrating consciousness of a single being dominates everything that is reported, the reader's mind must become caught up in the narrative for him to see the clear interaction between things, situations, and events."[16] The artist can depend on this technique to maintain the relationship between reader and text; the unifying narrative consciousness in such a work provides continuity for the reader. Therefore, it can be considered daring, and somewhat risky, that Cather does deviate from that single observing consciousness, which is Niel's in *A Lost Lady*. Wayne C. Booth points out that the use of the third-person "reflector" as he designates this technique is also invaluable for establishing the relationship between a character and the reader. He says:

> But it was not until we had discovered the full uses of the third person reflector that we found how to show a narrator changing *as he narrates*. . . . [T]he third person reflector can be shown, technically in the past tense but in effect present before our very eyes, moving toward or away from values that the reader holds dear.[17]

In using this technique, then, an author focuses attention on the development of the character through whose consciousness the action is perceived—the reader identifies with that character— and it is for this very reason that Cather devises another technique for revealing character. Niel Herbert is not the central figure in this story, although he is more than just a convenient spokesman. Cather's emphasis, like her focus, is on Marian Forrester. Niel's perception is, by far, the most significant perception that we have of Marian; it is in juxtaposition to Niel's romanticism, the identifying mark of his world view, that we see Marian's realism, the identifying characteristic of hers.[18] Niel's perception, however, can give the reader only one angle from which to see this heroine, and Cather wants the reader to see every side of her. Too much reader identification with Niel will defeat the purpose of the novel.

For this kind of reader response, therefore, Cather uses what we will call a multiple viewpoint point of view. Rather than limit her mode of reader information to Niel's center of consciousness, as James might do, she expands her options to include the viewpoints of those who perceive Marian differently, because those perceptions necessarily alter our own. By reserving the right to present scenes and events that are not available to Niel, Cather also allows for that "positioning" of Marian Forrester alone in the center of the table to be seen from all sides. When Cather chooses to show Marian and Frank's tryst through the eyes of Adolph Blum, she engages the reader in two ways. First, she maintains a consistently romantic point of view (Niel's) against which the reader can measure his or her own under-standing. Secondly, she sets up a relationship between Marian and Adolph Blum, which the reader must evaluate along with all the other relationships in the book. In this instance, we are observing Marian Forrester in a relationship with Frank Ellinger, which we are left to judge for ourselves, through the conscious-ness of a second young man who sees her in very different terms than Niel:

X Mrs. Forrester had never been too haughty to smile at him when he came to the back door with his fish. She never haggled about the price. She treated him like a human being. His little chats with her, her nod and smile when she passed him on the street, were among the pleasantest things he had to remember. She bought game of him in the closed season, and didn't give him away. (68)

In chapter 4, we demonstrated that the choice of point of view not only determines the manner in which information reaches the reader, it also determines the attitude of the reader toward the events of the novel. In *A Lost Lady,* Cather retains the ability to "position" her readers in relation to Marian Forrester by using a point of view which allows for the bifocal vision that is so char-acteristic of the modern sensibility. The reader is required to as-sess his or her own opinion in terms of the omniscient framing voice, in terms of Niel's limited vision, and in terms of those other angles of perception that we are given to complete the pic-ture. A vacuole exists between any two of those points of view and the authorial voice does not step in to fill it.[19]

In an article titled "Linearity and Fragmentation," Gabriel Josipovici makes the statement that "the nineteenth-century work *leaves no gaps.*" Far from the overfurnished nineteenth-century novels, in her own avant-garde work Willa Cather leaves vacuoles that the reader must fill to complete the story themati-cally and textually. Josipovici suggests that "the fragmentation of form we find in these literary works has much to do with Cub-ism and Serialism, that are all responses to the same needs, the same human needs, in particular the need to escape from what I call 'linearity.'"[20] In *A Lost Lady* we not only find a fragmenta-tion of Marian's total effect on other characters as we observe their various interchanges with her, but we are privy to Niel's internal fragmentation of his own view of her. He asks: "What did she do with all her exquisiteness when she was with a man like Ellinger? Where did she put it away?" (100).

Cather's ability to present her own modern bifocal vision of the world in a book with a single focus is extraordinary. Imposed on the story of Marian Forrester is the story of the decline of the pioneer spirit, but this second level of meaning never interferes with the reader's understanding of that central character. John Randall explains how Cather does so:

> In compact prose and in the brief space of 174 pages she manages to present as much as she ever could of what she felt to be the nature of life and the meaning of civilization, as well as give her interpretation of the history of an epic. The book is an excellent example of that kind of writing which is at the same time realistic and highly symbolic; the story runs along perfectly credibly on the literal level and yet every incident and almost every spoken word stands for more than itself and tells another tale. What Willa Cather has done is to present the story on two different levels, and much of the artistic beauty comes from the fact that in large measure the two are united, that action and significance, symbol and meaning, are one.[21]

This intricate juxtaposition of the past with the present is one of Cather's characteristically modern approaches to literature. As we have seen earlier, the sense that the modern world's complexity requires a constant evaluation of societal values marks the post–World War I writers as different from their nineteenth-century predecessors. Peter Faulkner sees their task as representing a world that is "especially more complex than the orderly world that had been presented to the reader in Victorian literature. The sense of complexity was to be the modernist writer's fundamental recognition."[22] That same sense of complexity is seen in A Lost Lady's form, which requires the accumulation of so much information before the reader can finally come to any conclusion in the absence of any authorial directive. The simplicity of the old order is seen in the rigidity of the social order, the structuring of roles, and the placidity of life. The authenticity of that ordered life constitutes its emotional appeal, and that accuracy of description comes from Cather's own experience. Captain Forrester remembers: "One day was like another, and all were glorious" (52); Willa Cather recalls: "While they were out on that sea of waving grass, one day was like another; and, if one can trust the memory of these old men, all the days were glorious."[23] The complexity of modern life is seen through Marian's confusion when her structure disintegrates; her blind and directionless course is prefigured by the image of the blinded female woodpecker desperately seeking shelter and survival. Although it has been frequently stated that Cather's portrayal of Marian is an indictment of modern values and a plea for a return to the old ways, we can also see this juxtaposition as a challenge to the reader. Because Cather maintains her authorial distance, the reader is invited to make his or her own assessment; nothing in the book condemns Marian for her behavior. Cather relies on the reader to supply what she has left unsaid, and she intentionally invites the reader's participation in constructing a value system. Wolfgang Iser explains that this kind of interaction results when a text employs the kind of blanks that arise "from the dense interweaving of perspectives, which cause a rapid and continued switch from theme to horizon."[24] Cather's handling of her theme against the horizon of her modern perspective thereby creates a vacuole in which the reader can also participate in that vision.

By refusing to pass judgment on Marian, Cather also aligns herself with another modern position. Harlan Hatcher tells us that "modernism was primarily a new set of values which contradicted the conventions of an outmoded past symbolized by the two themes which would later become quaintly synonymous, Puritanism and Victorianism."[25] There is a subtle but pervasive suggestion in the book that the relationship between men and women needs to be re-evaluated. For instance, Ivy refers to the woodpecker that he mutilates as "Miss Female" (23), Captain Forrester's pride in his cattle is equated with his pride in Marian (12), Niel refers to Constance as a "stubborn piece of pink flesh" (47), and Marian remarks, "Don't men like women to be different from themselves? They used to" (112). In the old order, Marian succeeds because she is different; in the modern world, she finds she must be the same—common, as Niel says (170).

In "Willa Cather's *A Lost Lady* and the Nineteenth-Century Novel of Adultery," Nancy Morrow explores this absence of authorial morality. Pointing out that *A Lost Lady* should follow the narrative pattern of earlier adultery novels, she illustrates how Cather "*changes* or reworks" these patterns.[26] This novel is not one about families, it is not about unhappy marriages, and it is not about Marian's religious background. Motherhood is simply not an issue.[27] What Morrow asserts is that "Niel's response to his own recognition of Marian's affair—his lack of concern for the *moral* implications of her actions—is the key to the novel's central intent and distinguishes *A Lost Lady* from earlier adultery novels."[28] We have established that the novel's central intent is the depiction of Marian Forrester. Therefore, it is not unrealistic to suspect that every technique that Cather employs has as its purpose the amplification of that characterization. Iser tells us that "it is typical of modern texts that they invoke expected functions in order to transform them into blanks. This is mostly brought about by a deliberate omission of generic features that have firmly been established by the tradition of the genre."[29] Although the reader might realistically entertain certain expectations in what he perceives as an "adultery novel," Cather refuses to meet those expectations, thereby forcing the reader to react in one way or another to Marian herself.[30]

Not only does Cather set up this contrast generically, she also uses the technique within the novel to involve her readers more intensely in the story. One of the most successful ways a writer can invest incidents with suggestiveness is to draw on those common systems of symbolism that we discussed in chapter 4. The reader unconsciously understands the implications of certain comparisons and all the associations of those particular symbols can be recalled by a brief reference. We have also seen that Cather can intensify those responses by using the symbol to represent the reverse of what is expected. In *A Lost Lady*, Cather does both. In chapter 2, part 1, the garden is most definitely Eden; it exists in all its pristine beauty complete with the "snake," Ivy Peters. In chapter 2, part 2, however, the garden is sterile and violated, even though the Captain points with pride to the sundial, which had its origins in the Garden of the Gods. Although Cather prepares the reader for Ivy Peters's wolfish avarice, it is Niel who wears a wolfskin jacket. Captain Forrester "values" his wife and his code of honor, but he leaves her destitute in a world where the only standard is monetary. Events and attitudes from part 1 are reworked in part 2; the reader must continually measure the impact of one against the other. The gracious dinner party of chapter 4, part 1, is parodied in chapter 8, part 2; Niel's proprietary attitude in the first part is mirrored by Ivy's access to Marian in the second; Judge Pommeroy's lament that "I've lived too long" (92) is refuted by Marian's determination to live.

As we have seen, Cather acknowledges her debt to Henry James by incorporating his theory and enlarging on his techniques in *A Lost Lady*. Here, too, she practices those lessons she has learned from Flaubert and demonstrates that she has elaborated on these as well. Pointing out similarities between their novels, David Stouck says:

More than one critic has drawn a parallel between *A Lost Lady* and Flaubert's *Emma Bovary*, but the importance of Niel to the novel creates closer parallels with *L'Education Sentimentale*. Frederic Moreau and Niel Herbert, both semi-orphaned and half-hearted law students, are subject to the treacheries of sex and beauty in a woman they romantically idealize. Both of the idealized women are married to men of declining means, and appearances are hard to maintain. One of the earliest images that both men associate with their romantic ideals is an ivory-handled parasol, and for both men a bouquet of roses thrown in the mud expresses disenchantment. The latter image might easily represent a direct borrowing by Willa Cather from Flaubert.[31]

It seems almost certain that the image of the roses *is* a direct borrowing, and, as such, represents Cather's own security with regard to her own artistic ability.[32] In "A Chance Meeting," which describes her encounter with Flaubert's niece Caroline, whom she meets as Madame Franklin Grout, Cather discusses *L'Education Sentimentale*. Her first reaction to the novel had been disappointment, but on rereading it, she recognized its greatness:

> It is something one has lived through, not a story one has read; less diverting than a story, perhaps, but more inevitable. One is "left with it," in the same way that one is left with a weak heart after certain illnesses. A shadow has come into one's consciousness that will not go out again.[33]

Its greatness for Cather lies in the fact that it fulfills her own criteria for art. Although Madame Grout dismisses Frederic as very weak and the book too long, she "spoke with warm affection" of Madame Arnoux. Indeed, Cather tells us:

> The niece had a very special feeling for this one of her uncle's characters. She lingered over the memory, recalling her as she first appears, sitting on the bench of a passenger boat on the Seine, in her muslin gown sprigged with green and her wide straw hat with red ribbons. Whenever the old lady mentioned Madame Arnoux it was with some mark of affection; she smiled, or sighed, or shook her head as we do when we speak of something that is quite unaccountably fine: "Ah yes, she is lovely, Madame Arnoux! She is very complete." (21).

It seems plausible, therefore, that Cather, with a mind full of literary material and a capacity for total recall, drew parallels for the sensitive reader that are reminiscent of the master from whom she had learned so much; she may have used Flaubert's "situation" and his imagery to demonstrate her own growth as an artist.[34] In *A Lost Lady* she pares away the dull parts, leaving only that central, vividly memorable figure who, like her predecessor, Madame Arnoux, can be conjured at will by the reader. Because her character is firmly based on Cather's own intense emotional experience of the effect a real woman had on her and others, every detail connected with Marian Forrester reinforces her authenticity. It is through the careful selection of detail, and the careful juxtaposition of those details, that Cather visualizes this character for her reader. It is from Flaubert that she learned to do so, and her novel is a tribute to him.

Flaubert once said: "What seems beautiful to me and what I should like to do is a book about nothing; a book with no exterior attachment."[35] In this sort of book, the language carries the entire weight of the composition; the author has no presence in the book. Therefore, each detail and image must add to the reader's understanding; the author must show what is happening without summarizing the action. This attitude results in the novel of concretized form, which we discussed earlier, and we can find examples of it in the clearly conceived and executed scenes of the book. The electricity in the scene between Marian and Frank Ellinger, captured in the image of white fingers clinging "to the black cloth as bits of paper cling to magnetized iron" (60), is viscerally "shocking" to the reader.

Edward and Lillian Bloom see compression, selectivity, and total relevance as essential tenets of Cather's style. They explain:

> The line that separated Willa Cather from most contemporary writers was enforced by her own attitude toward the nature and use of detail. It was an attitude developed out of an unconscious distinction between description and imagery. In her own novels she avoided objective description as much as possible because it is the physical, literal restatement of an actuality—and no more. Instead she relied heavily on the use of controlled imagery involving complexes of emotional and intellectual reactions, imagery conditioned by intimate participation.[36]

This assessment can be carried one step further if we consider the absolute necessity of maintaining that authorial distance of which we have spoken to elicit those emotional and intellectual reactions, which arise only from immediate and intense perception. The author must choose that detail or image or word that has the most resonance for the reader; the resonance of any element will depend on its relationship to the other elements of the text. Details are significant because they constitute images, and images are essential for the reader's participation in the story. The meaning that resides in the vacuole is the meaning that Cather intends because she controls the juxtaposition; the response that the reader makes is therefore also controlled by the writer. Iser's work with textual analysis considers this aspect of reader response to be an unconscious effect achieved by an author as he writes. Cather understood and used this principle consciously in order to write her book about nothing but ephemeral feminine charm.

Jonathan Raban identifies two techniques intensifying reader response that Cather uses in *A Lost Lady*. He says:

> When the novelist wants to attract attention to his images, to make us consider them as an integral part of his narrative, he has two main alternatives. Either he can repeat a particular image so often that its frequency constantly reminds us of its presence. Or he can extend it over a long passage, drawing parallels between his object and the thing with which it is compared. In both cases he will be giving his imagery an unusual and exaggerated weight.[37]

The extended image that immediately comes to mind in *A Lost Lady* is the comparison of Marian's decline with that of the pioneer spirit. Cather also draws parallels throughout the entire book to the creation myth, the garden of Eden, and the fall of man. By using these extended images, she maintains a unity underlying the many disparate details.

Cather's other way of maintaining unity through imagery is her repetition of images and of image systems. Marian Forrester's "long-lost lady laugh" (71) may well be her most identifying characteristic. Cather's re-creation of the effect of Marian's laughter is so striking a literary accomplishment that it produced a letter from F. Scott Fitzgerald explaining that he had written his description of Daisy in *The Great Gatsby* before he had read *A Lost Lady*, and he was concerned that she would think he had plagiarized. The letter is reprinted in Matthew J. Bruccoli's article, "'An Instance of Apparent Plagiarism': F. Scott Fitzgerald, Willa Cather, and the First *Gatsby* Manuscript," wherein Bruccoli reports:

On 28 April 1925 Willa Cather replied, saying that she had enjoyed reading *Gatsby* before she received Fitzgerald's letter and that she had not detected any duplication of *A Lost Lady*. She acknowledges that many authors have tried to say that same thing, but none has succeeded. The only way to describe beauty is to describe its effect, and not the person.[38]

Cather's description of the effect of Marian Forrester's charm is tied to the aural experience of her laughter. Incredibly, the reader has that experience through the language of the text.

Cather also uses jewels and flowers as recurrent images throughout the book, and we begin to suspect that she is here drawing on traditional systems of reference to underline her themes. For instance, Niel notices Marian's earrings of garnet and seed pearls. In the folklore of gems, garnets represent love's constancy and pearls are the emblem of modesty and purity, all attributes that Neil would assign to Mrs. Forrester. When Niel listens to Marian's conversation with Ellinger after she learns of his marriage, he imagines her voice "like the color in an opal" (133), which symbolizes bad luck.[39]

Marian's rings are mentioned often, not to emphasize her marital fidelity to Captain Forrester but rather to indicate her infidelity with Frank Ellinger. The rings are more significant in their absence than in their essence. The Captain's fascination with jewels and his belief that a woman must be worthy of them elicit an unwritten, but suggested, comparison of this story with that of the biblical pearl of great price. Is Marian the "jewel" sacrificed to the Captain's honor?

Flower imagery is abundant and specific, beginning with the names of the characters: Niel *Herbert*, Marian and Daniel *Forrester*, *Ivy* Peters. Enough evidence exists to assume that Cather refers to the Victorian language of the flowers when she chooses specific kinds at specific moments. Roses, which appear most frequently and in many varieties, stand for love. Pink roses, which Marian arranges in the second chapter, are the symbol of simplicity, and the idyllic picture of the world as Paradise is a vision of a simpler time. Wild roses, the Captain's roses, briar roses, roses with thorns, and the yellow roses of jealousy that Adolph Blum brings to Marian on the day of Captain Forrester's funeral—all accumulate to an ultimate image of love ultimately lost. Perhaps the most interesting use of roses is the juxtaposition of June roses with mock orange in chapter 8. As the Captain returns home to tell Marian that he is a ruined man, the mere mention of the fragrance from these two flowers suggests weddings, marriages, and mockeries.[40]

Any contemporary of Cather's would also know that the comparison of Marian's complexion to white lilacs refers to its youthful innocence, and the change in it which reminds Niel of ivory gardenias signifies a secret untold love. The imagery thus works on as many levels as the reader can accommodate. Knowing what the flowers represent does not determine meaning for any reader; the metaphor stands on its own. If the reader can bring to the symbol an added dimension, however, the imagery necessarily suggests more than is written on the page.

James Woodress comments that in *A Lost Lady* "Cather makes no effort to supply a continuous narrative but skips seven years between chapters two and three."[41] As we have seen, it is not Cather's intention to write a book that requires a continuous narrative. In fact, fragmentation and juxtaposition are the methods by which she tells the story. In this novel, which repays her debts to James and Flaubert, Cather relies on an unobtrusive yet symmetrical structure that unifies the book and integrates the many juxtapositions within the text, an intricate system of imagery through which she draws on her readers' subconscious associative capacity to enrich their comprehension of both the action of the plot and the characters involved therein. Cather is confident that her reader will cooperate by reading with a sensitivity to the information *not* supplied in the text, thereby ensuring that the central focus of the book, the impression of one character on the reader, is that fine residue that remains when the story is over. More than a character sketch, *A Lost Lady* demonstrates Willa Cather's command of techniques which result in a deceptively simple book that evokes an intensely complex reaction. We have seen that the book can be read as allegory; that it represents a surprisingly ambiguous, perhaps even amoral, attitude toward convention; and that it reverberates with a passion not explicitly depicted in its pages, but suggested through both familiar and esoteric imagery. Although we are limiting our discussion of *A Lost Lady* to those techniques that make possible such a range of readings, we must acknowledge the many directions in which productive study can proceed. In this work, Cather demonstrates that she has developed her own techniques and style, evolving from, but also different from, those that James and Flaubert taught her. Willa Cather's experiments in this novel deal with her handling of the vacuole in a tightly structured, yet organic, form and her manipulation of her readers through their willingness to join those vacuoles within the structure of the story. In her next novel, *The Professor's House*, this experimentation takes a more radical direction in which she uses juxtaposition as a structuring concept as well as a literary technique: she carefully places vacuoles for maximum reader involvement, explores the uses of time and memory, and provides a self-conscious gloss on the creative springs of her own imagination.

6

The Professor's House: An Experiment in the Use of Time, Memory, and Juxtaposition

If *A Lost Lady* was Willa Cather's most popular book, then *The Professor's House* may very well be her most perplexing and most discussed. Many early critics found fault with the book's experimental structure, disconcerted by the abrupt break in the continuity of the story. Lionel Trilling approves of the theme of the book, which he identifies as the failure of the pioneer spirit in the wider field of American life and finally decides outweighs its defects. He says, however: "Lame as it is, it epitomizes as well as any novel of our time the disgust with life which so many sensitive Americans feel."[1] Joseph Wood Krutch titled his review of *The Professor's House* "Second Best," calling it "fragmentary and inconclusive," and regretfully deciding that "the book is a disappointment to those who know how good her best work can be."[2] Although Alfred Kazin says that *The Professor's House* is "the most persistently underrated" of Cather's novels, he too, finds its form disturbing:

> Actually it is one of those imperfect and ambitious books whose very imperfections illuminate the quality of an imagination. . . . The violence with which she broke the book in half to tell the long and discursive narrative of Tom Outland's boyhood in the Southwest was a technical mistake that has damned the book, but the work itself as a whole is the most brilliant statement of her endeavor as an artist.[3]

Since 1970, however, the novel has attracted a great deal of academic attention; it appeared in paperback in 1973, and we have now an impressive accumulation of scholarly and factual information dealing with the literary antecedents, the generic analogies with art and music, and the biographical stories that illuminate our understanding of this difficult book.

Merrill Maguire Skaggs proposes that we consider the book as the first of a "four novel span of works exploring the relationship between art and religion" but begins with the premise that "it now seems clear that she tried an unusual experimental form, in order to gain specific special effects."[4] Indeed, it seems foolhardy to discuss *The Professor's House* without considering the book's form and the effect of that form on the reader. In this study, we shall focus on those technical aspects of Cather's experimental *Professor's House* such as the use of juxtaposition, the excision of all but essential and telling detail, and the careful placement of vacuoles. Cather herself comments on the book's structure twice in print. When Elizabeth Moorhead recalls her own admiration for the novel after rereading it in 1940, she remembers that Cather appreciated a favorable reaction to the book and that she explained her initial idea for the book's form:

> I am always glad to hear a good word for *The Professor's House*, which has been, I suspect, the least popular of the books you mention. To most people, I think, it is just "another story." But to me it was an interesting experiment. I really got the idea from a Dutch painting: a rich warm interior—and through an open window the sea, blue, very much alive, with a light wind on the water. I tried to use the Blue Mesa in that particular way, but most people seem to think it was a very faulty kind of structure.[5]

In chapter 2, we noted Cather's description of the two experiments in form, which she said she was trying with the novel: one, to insert the *Nouvelle* into the *Roman* and the other, to follow the arrangement of the sonata form. In this earlier letter, Cather also recounts her reaction to the Dutch painting, and states her intention of reproducing that same effect with this book. She writes:

> Just before I began the book I had seen, in Paris, an exhibition of old and modern Dutch paintings. In many of them the scene presented was a living-room warmly furnished, or a kitchen full of food and coppers. But in most of the interiors, whether drawingroom or kitchen, there was a square window, open, through which one saw masts of ships, or a stretch of grey sea. The feeling of the sea that one got through those square windows was remarkable.[6]

Of course, what we must note is that Cather is describing the effect of juxtaposition on the perceiving eye. The "feeling" of the sea is made more intense because the sea is seen in the context of the crowded room; it is, in effect, surrounded by the room.[7] Cather continues:

> In my book I tried to make Professor St. Peter's house rather over-crowded and stuffy with new things; American proprieties, clothes, furs, petty ambitions, quivering jealousies—until one got rather stifled. Then I wanted to open the square window and let in the fresh air that blew off the Blue Mesa, and the fine disregard of trivialities which was in Tom Outland's face and in his behaviour.[8]

By juxtaposing the primitive and beautiful Southwest with the stuffy houses of Hamilton, Cather elicits a response from the reader that forces an evaluation of each and its effect on the other. By surrounding the Blue Mesa with the overcrowded lives of the Professor and his family, she intensifies the contrast twice. We might suggest that she constructs the story of the Professor, then fills the vacuole between the two parts for us so that we have the same images impinging one on the other as we proceed from fragmented intuition to an understanding whole. Just as the three movements of a sonata require three mood changes that contribute to a total effect, the three parts of *The Professor's House* require of the reader the same sensitivity to mood. Just as the *Nouvelle* comments on the *Roman*, the narrative of Tom Outland's experience comments on the novel as a whole.[9] The principle of juxtaposition, which we have seen operating internally within Cather's works, is itself the structuring idea from which *The Professor's House* is made.

Peter Ackroyd, wrestling with the concept of the modern in his book *Notes for a New Culture,* considers a definition:

> How is modernism to be best expressed? Perhaps it can best be described as a sense of freedom. We no longer invest created forms with our own significance and, in parallel, we no longer seek to interpret our lives in factitious terms of art. Artistic forms are no longer to be conceived of as paradigmatic or mimetic.[10]

If the modern attitude is demonstrated by this sense of freedom, then Cather's choice of this radically different form can be seen as a modern experiment. By this time in her career, she has attained the confidence to use any method available to her to evoke the desired response. Lillian and Edward Bloom consider

Cather's choice of form as an artistic necessity dictated by her expanding conviction that form must follow concept:

> Quite clearly *The Professor's House* is not only an experimental novel but one that is successfully so. And quite as clearly when Willa Cather announced her hostility toward invention, she meant what we would call contrivance or the forced manipulation of plot and character. Behind such overt hostility was her view of structure as a necessary—hence natural—outcome of an idea that had germinated long before the birth of the fabric itself. And if the idea or concept can best be expressed by a form that is new rather than traditional, then the novelist has no choice—he must try the new.[11]

Given her own explanation of what she was trying to do, then, we must look at the work in terms of how successfully she manages to create that same gasp of recognition in her reader that she herself experienced as she looked at the sea through the window of a crowded room.[12]

The Professor's House is an excellent example of Willa Cather's ability to arouse her reader's emotional response by manipulation through juxtaposition, to create art out of memory while explaining how it is done, and to experiment with new modes of expression that have become standard twentieth-century procedure, and that we attribute to the modernist influence. In this work, Cather invites her reader's closest attention, for the plot is not complete until the end and information is meted out in fragmentary form. Here, too, she invests the Professor with her own acute and intense capacity of observation. In this novel, she abandons chronological security, bows to Marcel Proust, and weaves an intricate work in which Time is constantly shifting.

David Daiches points out that *The Professor's House* is "Miss Cather's first full treatment of a theme which has become so important in the twentieth-century novel, the first of her novels which links her, however, tenuously to what might be called the modern novel of sensibility so successfully practiced in England by Virginia Woolf and still very much alive."[13] We can agree that *The Professor's House* is "modern" in its theme; surely the disenchanted and disillusioned Professor is a twentieth-century man finding his way through the waste land. We must remember, however, that Willa Cather has a far more complicated world view than many of her younger contemporaries, because she has an innate sense of tradition that we have noted, as well as a sense of modern chaos, and is able to see the present in juxtaposition with the past. As Patricia Yongue reminds us:

There is . . . an important aspect of Willa Cather's use of time and the past, as well as of her theory of art, that comes out of a close examination of her fiction and her non-fiction. It is an aspect that has been neglected primarily by the critics of the "death-wish school" who have not seen what Willa Cather most clearly saw—the artistic value of the historical past and the use of it to illuminate the present rather than to ignore it.[14]

We have seen that Cather contrasts the not-so-distant past with the present in *A Lost Lady*. In *The Professor's House*, as in *The Song of the Lark*, she returns to the prehistoric and heroic time of the Ancient People, the Cliff Dwellers. Cather is not the only writer of her day to look at the present in terms of the country's course of history.[15] Ezra Pound, T. S. Eliot, Gertrude Stein, and William Carlos Williams all dealt with the declining values of American society. Cather's perspective, however, marks her attitude as different from theirs, and her Professor is therefore a different kind of hero.[16] As Philip Gerber points out:

Willa Cather was not completely out of step with the writers of her era, but the difference is tremendous. From her waste land there rises always the Rock, strong, defiant, reaching for the clouds to postulate all the affirmative virtues of character, fidelity, idealism, civilization, culture, religion, ethics, and order, standing as Miss Cather would express it, like a Tanagra figurine among Kewpie dolls.[17]

By putting her Rock—the Blue Mesa—squarely in the center of her novel, everything else must be seen in relation—or in juxtaposition—to it. Professor St. Peter measures his family in terms of the Rock, but he, too, must be seen in relation to those values that it represents. As Edward Wagenknecht reminds us: "As passionately as any of the moderns, Willa Cather believed in the fulfillment of individual destiny. But her people have roots and she does not present fulfillment in terms of a shrinking of responsibility."[18]

Eudora Welty has suggested that the origin of Cather's technique of juxtaposition lies in her childhood move from Virginia to Nebraska. She proposes that Cather

worked out some of her most significant effects by bringing widely separated lives, times, experiences together—placing them side by side or one within the other, opening out of it almost like a vision—like Tom Outland's story from *The Professor's House*—or existing along with it, waiting in its path, like the mirage.[19]

In this novel, as indicated earlier, Cather uses juxtaposition to position the vacuoles for maximum reader involvement, demonstrating that she understood the principles now being advanced by reader-response theorists with regard to the importance of the vacuole in the juxtaposition of two images. We have already mentioned the notion that the whole of Tom Outland's Story can be seen as an illustration of how a vacuole actually works. Here, Cather interrupts the continuation of her story, creating a gap within the progression of events taking place in "present" time. Because Cather cannot expect even sensitive readers to bring to the story her own experience of the Old Southwest, she gives them that intense emotional reaction to the Cliff Dwellers that she herself experienced when she first visited the Southwest. Tom Outland's Story is filled with information that directly alters the reader's perception of the St. Peter family and its relationships; once readers have also made this experience their own, the events of both books 1 and 3 are altered. Interestingly, the primary juxtaposition is not between the past of Tom's experience and the present, but between the past that Tom has constructed from the evidence of the Blue Mesa and the present. Tom's story itself is full of petty ambition, such as that he sees in Washington, and double betrayal—just as Roddy betrays Tom by selling the artifacts, Tom in turn betrays his friend by casting him out into the night. Lest we miss this point, Cather has Tom say, "But the older I grow, the more I understand what it was I did that night on the mesa. Anyone who requites faith and friendship as I did, will have to pay for it."[20] Welty is again helpful in understanding the mechanics of this particular vacuole. She says:

> The Professor's House is a novel with a unique form, and to read it is to see it built before our eyes: the making of two unlike parts into a whole under a sheltering third part which defines it and is as final as that verse that comes to recite itself to the Professor's mind. The construction is simple, forthright and daring. By bringing the Professor's old house and the Cliff Dweller's house in combination to the mind, Willa Cather gives them simultaneous existence, and with the measure of time taken away, we may see, in the way of a mirage, or a vision, humanity's dwelling places all brought into one.[21]

What happens as well is that the reader also reacts to Tom's experiences in juxtaposition to the story of the Cliff Dwellers and in terms of subsequent events, which the reader knows from book 1. The effect is intensified as the reader begins book 3; because the events of book 1 have been altered by book 2, events and facts that were assimilated must be reevaluated as they appear again and as they impinge on one another. Wolfgang Iser also identifies this structuring process as a means of manipulating the reader:

> Impeded image building compels us to give up images we have formed for ourselves, so that we are maneuvered into a position outside our own products and are thus led to produce images which, with our habitual way of thinking we could not have conceived.[22]

He continues by explaining that the vacuole—or blank, as he calls it—is responsible for the reader's ability to respond fully to the text:

> The blank in the fictional text appears to be a paradigmatic structure; its function consists in initiating structured operations in the reader, the execution of which transmits the reciprocal interaction of textual positions into consciousness. The shifting blank is responsible for a sequence of colliding images which condition each other in the time-flow of reading. The discarded image imprints itself on its successor, even though the latter is meant to resolve the deficiencies of the former. In this respect, the images hang together in a sequence, and it is by this sequence the meaning of the text comes alive in the reader's imagination.[23]

Lillian's hostility to Tom Outland, visible at the beginning of the book, must be reassessed in terms of her initial hospitality and warmth; in fact, we discover that the Professor was rather skeptical of Tom at first, whereas Lillian, Rosamond and, especially, Kathleen were welcoming and interested in the fascinating stranger. The personal relationship between Rosamond and Tom is nebulous; we know that Tom asked her to the Senior Dance, that they became engaged, and that he left his patent to her in his will. We certainly know nothing about Rosamond's emotional attachment to Tom, nor really anything about his to her. We do know that some unwritten story exists in the vacuoles of Kathleen's relationship to Tom. Cather intends to evoke the reader's speculation. We learn more about Tom from Kathleen than from any other character; we never fully accept money as the reason for the sisters' estrangement; and we are left to invent any number of explanations for the scene between Kathleen and

Scott in which she insists: "You know you *are* the real one, don't you?" (110).

Cather manages to create in the reader a suspension of judgment with regard to the characters and events of the story by constantly shifting the perspective as both characters and events are seen in different relationships, juxtaposed in new combinations. Every character in the book can be defined in terms of his or her relationship to the dead Tom Outland, but every character must also be defined in terms of his or her relationship to the Professor as well. The Professor ponders this phenomenon of shifting perceptions when he considers his wife in terms of Louie:

> Mrs. St. Peter was wearing the white silk crepe that had been the most successful of her summer dresses, and an orchid velvet ribbon about her shining hair. She wouldn't have made herself look quite so well if Louie hadn't been coming, he reflected. Or was it that he wouldn't have noticed if Louie hadn't been there? A man long accustomed to admire his wife in general, seldom pauses to admire her in a particular gown or attitude, unless his attention is directed to her by the appreciative gaze of another man. (77–78)

In "The Reading of Fictional Texts," Karlheinz Stierle maintains that the distinctive feature of fiction is "its ability to articulate a system of perspectives." He argues that the text sets up a relationship of theme and horizon that is itself the actual "subject" or "theme" of the work, that "not as reality, but as nonreality does fiction provide its own possibility for ordering experience." He continues:

> Creative fiction writing establishes, or at least experiments with, new systems of perspectives. The world of fiction is a competitive world of new views and new ways of presenting them. We may thus think of fiction as shaping the horizon of our everyday life by providing us with new models for the organization of our experience.[24]

We see, then, that Willa Cather uses juxtaposition to establish a number of different perspectives for the reader. She uses the Cliff Dwellers as the horizon against which later experiences are seen; therefore the text contains within itself the standard by which we are to measure all further activity. Cather once said: "Art requires a vast amount of character. It's a whole lot more important than talent. It demonstrates itself in relationships the artist thinks important."[25] Here the shifting relationships among the characters, with their attendant vacuoles, require from the reader a constant participation in the construction of the "nonreality" of the novel itself. Out of those relationships that Cather thinks are important comes the written and unwritten story that together constitute the work of art.

The Professor tells his class: "Art and religion (they are the same thing, in the end, of course), have given man the only happiness he has ever had" (69). St. Peter—and Willa Cather—believe that the individual needs ritual, order, mystery, and life colored by imagination. As Cather creates this made work of art, as she turns the reality of her own experience into the unreality of fiction, she also divulges the process by which she is able to do so. Much has been made of the Professor as an alter ego for Cather in her mid-life crisis; one can find parallels of age, productivity, success, and prestige. Cather also gives the Professor some of her own experiences that directly relate to her growth as a writer. Cather describes the effect of her own devastating move from Virginia to Nebraska in St. Peter's wrenching move from the lakeside to Kansas when he, too, was eight: "It was like sinking for the third time" (31). She gives him the same problem with the critics: "Nobody saw that he was trying to do something quite different—they merely thought he was trying to do the usual thing, and had not succeeded very well" (32). Finally, she gives her Professor that same explosion of understanding she had when she recognized that would be the inevitable design of *O Pioneers!*

> St. Peter lay looking up at them from a little boat riding low in the purple water, and the design of his book unfolded in the air above him, just as definitely as the mountain ranges themselves. And the design was sound. He had accepted it as inevitable, had never meddled with it, and it had seen him through. (106)

Also evident throughout the book are those peculiarities of observation in St. Peter that, in Cather, make her an artist.

Cather attributes her ability to recreate scenes from her memory to the fact that they are remarkably clear to her in all their emotional intensity. Her words bear repeating in this context: "When we have a vivid experience in social intercourse, pleasant or unpleasant, it records itself in our memory in the form of a scene; and when it flashes back to us, all sorts of apparently unimportant details are flashed back with it."[26] With the Professor, she shows us just what she means:

> When the ice chunks came in of a winter morning, crumbly and white, throwing off gold and rose-coloured reflections from a copper-coloured sun behind the grey clouds, he didn't observe the detail or know what it was that made him happy, but now, forty years later, he could recall all its aspects perfectly. They had made pictures in him when he was willing and unconscious, when his eyes were merely wide open. (30)

We must remember that Cather maintained, "most of the material a writer works with is acquired before the age of fifteen."

In "Defoe's *The Fortunate Mistress*," Cather says: "Defoe is a writer of ready invention but no imagination—with none of the personal attributes which, fused together somehow, make imagination."[27] As she told Ethel Hockett in 1915, "Imagination, which is a quality writers must have, does not mean the ability to weave pretty stories out of nothing. In the right sense, imagination is a response to what is going on—a sensitiveness to which outside things appeal. It is a composition of sympathy and observation."[28] This distinction between invention and imagination is crucial to an understanding of Cather's principle of selection. Thomas Uzzell says:

> Invention is sorting out, selecting, combining objects, people and things, together with prescriptions for new qualities to be given the object in the full treatment of writing. Invention is a rearrangement of existing things, while imagination gives existing things new qualities.[29]

For Cather, then, imaginative ability to give existing things new qualities arises from the artist's "gift of sympathy" and his or her powers of observation. Once the artist has observed and absorbed, however, his or her task is to choose, to select, to arrange. It is useful to recall here the quotation from Mérimée cited by Cather in "The Novel Démeublé": "The art of choosing among the innumerable strokes which nature offers us is, after all, much more difficult than that of observing them with attention and describing them with exactitude" (my translation).[30] Professor St. Peter makes the same observation:

> He left the walk and cut across the turf, intending to enter by the French window, but he paused a moment to admire the scene within. The drawing-room was full of autumn flowers, dahlias and wild asters and golden-rod. The red-gold sunlight lay in bright puddles on the thick blue carpet, made hazy aureoles about the stuffed blue

chairs. There was, in the room, as he looked through the window, a rich intense effect of autumn, something that presented October much more sharply and sweetly to him than the coloured maples and the aster-bordered paths by which he had come home. It struck him that the seasons sometimes gain by being brought into the house, just as they gain by being brought into painting, and into poetry. The hand, fastidious and bold, which selected and placed—it was that which made the difference. In Nature there is no selection. (75)

We must note that in this passage Cather reverses her own image; St. Peter, standing on the outside, looking at the interior room framed like a painting by the window, has an intense experience of October mirroring Cather's experience of the sea as she looked at the Dutch painting from inside a room. For Cather, art must create an impression of reality, not reality itself, for that it cannot do, and the artist successfully does so only by choosing those details that imagination can arrange into a satisfying and telling whole.

We earlier mentioned that Cather's style involves the use of strong verbs, many figures of speech, and color to express great emotion. We see these characteristics in both of the passages we have considered here, but in this book, Cather actually describes for her reader what her style is like and what its effect is supposed to have. The Professor reflects on the clarity of style with which Tom Outland wrote his diary:

To St. Peter this plain account was almost beautiful, because of the stupidities it avoided and the things it did not say. If words had cost money, Tom couldn't have used them more sparingly. The adjectives were purely descriptive, relating to form and color, and were used to present the objects under consideration, not the young explorer's emotions. Yet though this austerity one felt the kindling imagination, the ardour and excitement of the boy, like the vibration in a voice when the speaker tries to conceal his emotions by using only conventional phrases. (262–63)

Willa wrote to her old friend Irene Miner Weisz, who had seen *The Professor's House* in its early stages, to tell her that she was pleased that Irene had got the really fierce feeling that lay behind the rather dry and impersonal manner of the telling.[31] Behind all of Cather's work is that fierce feeling that defies explanation or explication but is transmitted to the reader by these very clearly defined technical methods, which make Tom Outland's writing so moving.

In 1913, Marcel Proust privately published *Swann's Way*, the first volume of his seven-volume masterpiece, *Remembrance of Things Past*. Cather's avid interest in her French contemporaries is recorded by Elizabeth Sergeant, who remembers bringing Cather books by André Gide as well as others. Sergeant specifically recalls:

> I had also brought her a couple of volumes of a "new" French writer of whom I'd first heard in Parc from Jean Giraudoux. He was named Marcel Proust. . . . Willa was always happy to know of new French authors whom she preferred to new American writers.[32]

Because memory and time play such an important role in *The Professor's House* and because we know that Cather was familiar with Proust's work, it is not unreasonable to look for parallels between these two great modern writers.[33] In discussing the uses of memory in Cather, Louis Kronenberger refers to Proust to suggest differences rather than similarities. He says:

> Her memory is of more than utilitarian value to her; it is the instrument through which all the notes of these are blown, and it sets the tone for them. The memory-sense and the time-sense play as great a part and command as peculiar an effect with Willa Cather as in a different way they do with Proust.[34]

Certainly we have demonstrated that memory is central to Cather's art; she said, "Life began for me when I ceased to admire and began to remember."[35] In the broadest sense, we can apply this to Sarah Orne Jewett's insistence that Cather search her own memory for "the thing that teases the mind,"[36] but in a far more narrow sense we can apply this statement to both Proust's narrator and to the Professor himself. When Proust's young man bites into the *madeleine* cake and experiences that intense childhood memory which releases him from his sense of despair and enables him to write the book which we are reading, he is also acknowledging that he begins to live again. When the Professor commits himself to life without delight after remembering all the delights of childhood, he too is beginning again.[37]

The whole of *The Professor's House* is seen in terms of memory: Tom Outland is merely a memory, only "a glittering idea" perhaps; the early years of the Professor's marriage and his creative years are also a memory; and the Cliff Dwellers are reconstructed and remembered through the artifacts they left. Part of the tremendous contrast between books 1 and 2 is the shift from third person, which is distancing and allows for a certain nostalgic tone, to the first-person narrator, which requires a different reaction from the reader. We do not register at first, however, that Tom is speaking after the fact; everything that he says is also colored by nostalgia and imperfect memory.

In "Modern Literature and the Sense of Time," W. T. Noon points out that "the technical problem of time in a narrative—foreshortening, perspective, acceleration, tempo, and so forth—permits of many complex and sophisticated resolutions by poets and novelists."[38] As we have seen, Cather solves many of her time problems by juxtaposition, intentionally creating reader-involving vacuoles. The Professor's memory of the rainy holiday in Paris is succeeded by his return to his first days in France and then interrupted by the summer he spent in Spain. Louis Giannetti refers to this technique, used successfully by film makers and borrowed from literature, as "mixed flashbacks."[39] Peter Ackroyd says further that "since meaning is being continually created, it takes a complete reading of the text to uncover this continual accumulation and shifting of meaning, and it eventually creates a sense of a world which stands apart from our own efforts to impart significance to it."[40]

In *The Professor's House,* Cather complicates the issue of time even further by playing out the actions of her characters against the larger scope of time which stretches back past the Cliff Dwellers and, conversely, forward beyond St. Peter's future. Edwin Muir differentiates between the use of time in a dramatic novel and in what he defines as the chronicle. He says:

> Time in the dramatic novel is internal; its movement is the movement of the figures; change, fate and character are all condensed into one action; and with its resolution there comes a pause in which time seems to stand still; the arena is left vacant. In the chronicle, on the other hand, time is eternal; it is not seized subjectively and humanly in the minds of the characters; it is seen from a fixed Newtonian point outside. It flows past the beholder; it flows over and through the figure he evokes. Instead of narrowing to a point, the point fixed by passion, or fear, or fate in the dramatic novel, it stretches away indefinitely, running with a scarcely perceptible check over all the barriers which might have marked its end.[41]

In a second reversal, Cather presents the "eternal" time of Tom Outland's story in the first-person conversational tone and the defined time of the dramatic books in a more distancing third-person narration. Time flows without check beneath the surface of this novel; Cather's experimental use of these differing concepts of time in juxtaposition heightens the effect of each and again directs the reader to a deeper appreciation of the philosophical whole, which they necessarily constitute.

In *Symbol and Metaphor in Human Experience*, Martin Foss observes:

> Art has its own reality, which is not the reality of the object but of the creative process. Reality does not reside in the words, fixed and connected in sentences of a poem; not even in the scenes or acts of a drama as they stand out in detached objectivity. Reality does not reside in the togetherness of colors on the canvas or the multitude of consonant and dissonant sounds of music. All these objective entities are necessary, but they are not real. They have to be known, have to be put into a composition which is made and can be explained.[42]

In this book, Cather experiments with a form that will require the reader's participation in that creative process. Using juxtaposition as a structuring concept, she relies on the habit of the mind that constructs wholeness out of parts; she elicits from her readers a willingness to discard the partial whole in favor of a more completed unity. By participating in the construction of the reality that is the work of art, the reader has also experienced the emotional component of creation.

J. Bronowski writes in *Science and Human Values*:

> When a simile takes us aback and persuades us altogether, when we find a juxtaposition in a picture both odd and intriguing, when a theory is at once fresh and convincing, we do not merely nod over someone else's work. We re-enact the creative act, and we ourselves make the discovery again. At bottom there is no unifying likeness there until we too have made it for ourselves.[43]

Through experience and experimentation, Willa Cather found this point to be true and proved it with *The Professor's House*. She relied on juxtaposition as a structuring principle as well as a literary technique, used time and memory with the same coincidence they appear to have within the human consciousness, and constructed a work of art that stands as a made thing—a fictional reality—reproducing the effect of life as it contains within itself that self-conscious explanation of its own methods.

7

My Mortal Enemy: The Novel Démeublé

As we have seen, Willa Cather had proposed a new approach to the art of writing that challenged the naturalistic methods of the time, when, in her 1922 essay "The Novel Démeublé," she declared:

> How wonderful if we could throw all the furniture out of the window; and along with it, all the meaningless reiterations concerning physical sensations, all the tiresome old patterns, and leave the room as bare as the stage of a Greek theatre, or as that house into which the glory of Pentecost descended; leave the scene bare for the play of emotions, great and little—for the nursery tale, no less than the tragedy, is killed by tasteless amplitude. The elder Dumas enunciated a great principle when he said that to make a drama, a man needed one passion, and four walls.[1]

Having stated her minimalist position, she then proceeded to demonstrate the principle with increasing compression and economy in the books of her middle years. Thus, we have been able to demonstrate that *A Lost Lady* and *The Professor's House* represent different experiments using techniques she developed to evoke a story that is "felt upon the page without being specifically named there."[2] As we shall see in this chapter, with *My Mortal Enemy*, she abandons all literary ornament, and using the reader-involving techniques she has perfected in the preceding novels—carefully managed point of view, juxtaposition, excision, and complex imagery—she writes the quintessential novel *démeublé*, proving Dumas's principle right by limiting herself to one passion, and very little more than four walls. As E. K. Brown says:

> It is the boldest experiment she had ever made in leaving out, in the subordination of secondary characters, the reduction of settings to where "they seemed to exist, not so much in the author's mind, as

in the emotional penumbra of the characters themselves." Nothing distracts from the rendering of Myra herself, least of all the style, fluid and transparent beyond anything Willa Cather had accomplished.[3]

Here we find that Cather's style has become that apparently effortless medium through which the artist creates a work of art that succeeds. And we must remember that "the absolute necessity in art is the personal encounter. The work of art succeeds if something works—if there is a response."[4]

Critical response to *My Mortal Enemy* has ranged from puzzlement to disdain to enthusiastic approval. James Woodress calls *My Mortal Enemy* "the most bitter piece of fiction" Cather ever wrote.[5] John Randall says it is "the most bizarre of Willa Cather's books," as well as the "least likable."[6] Lina Mainiero suggests that this is Cather's "most mysterious work" that "derives its impact from what remains unsaid, from depths that seem constantly to be assaultng the cool surface."[7] David Stouck represents one response to the book: "My reading of the novel is perhaps best approached through the title,"[8] and his assessment of the book, like many others, centers on discovering Myra's real enemy.[9] Ellen Moers responds to the mother-daughter conflict she sees between Myra and Nellie, and she makes an interesting observation that illustrates Cather's habit of reversing reader expectations. She proposes:

> In modern times the mother-daughter relationship which lies at the base of educating heroinism undergoes a characteristic twist: now it is not the parents but the child's viewpoint which dominates. The controlling literary consciousness is that of the subject of matriarchal authority, its enraged victim, its adoring slave. Someone like Willa Cather's Nellie Birdseye.[10]

Merrill Maguire Skaggs describes the intricate "triangulated" relationship entangling Myra, Nellie, and Oswald.[11] Philip Gerber considers the book the converse of *My Ántonia*.[12] Susan Rosowski calls the book Cather's version of an awakening, adding, "In stripping away conventions to reach a meaning so individual that each character—and each reader—must discover it for himself or herself, Cather anticipates later writers who would similarly work towards questions rather than answers."[13] The number of responses to this book is determined by the number of readers it has had, and this book has enjoyed a large audience well beyond the academic sphere.[14] Cather's work of art succeeds because she succeeds in evoking her readers' response to the complex and profound story that exists beyond the brief 105 pages of text.

In this book we find all those techniques that Willa Cather has honed in order to trigger that sudden explosion of understanding which is the mark of real art. Cather practices exactly what she preaches in *My Mortal Enemy*; she sets herself strict limits, and, within those boundaries, she manipulates her few and select details to produce a story that is not named specifically on the page but that has the quality she sought in everything she wrote: "A quality which one can remember without the volume at hand, can experience over and over in the mind but can never absolutely define."[15] Using her readers' common intellectual background, a multiple viewpoint point of view that differs from the one she used in *A Lost Lady*, and internal juxtaposition that produces reader-controlling vacuoles, she demonstrates her mastery of these modern techniques with a style so pure and seamless that none of them is obtrusive or evident.

Josephine Jessup believes that "*My Mortal Enemy* (1926) shows even greater elaboration of aesthetic detail than *A Lost Lady*. Vignettes on religion, opera, poetry and the drama appear as a succession of exquisitely embroidered screens behind the gaunt action of the center stage."[16] Because there are so few details, every one must count; each carries the full weight of the reference because no final accumulation of effects occurs. We have earlier seen how the aria *Casta diva* comments explicitly on Myra's character; as Richard Giannone points out, the aria reveals Norma's duplicity: "What starts as a prayer for peace . . . ends as a cry for vengeance."[17] The Schubert air that Nellie hears as she unpacks in the dreary apartment-hotel is the promise of happy times to come, says Giannone, and represents all that Myra has lost.[18] We might also suggest, however, that it represents all that Nellie has to gain.

References to poetry abound throughout *My Mortal Enemy*; we should remember that poetry is the most compressed form of literature. Myra writes poems for Ewan to give to Esther, she is also a friend of the poet Ann Aylward, and poetry has played an important part in her own courtship. Cather mentions Heine, whose anachronistic tear Myra sheds, and Whitman, "that dirty old man" who just might get Myra into Parnassus where another dirty old man, her uncle, has been "translated, with no dark conclusion to the pageant, no 'night of the grave'"(18). Shakespeare is mentioned three times in the novel; references to *Hamlet*, the history plays *Richard II* and *King John*, and *King Lear* deepen our understanding of the story without adding to its bulk. David Stouck says that "the refrence to *Hamlet* played by Sarah Bernhardt not only reflects the confusion of sexual roles in the Henshawe menage, but the painful uncertainty of the narrator as well."[19] Harry B. Eichorn says, "By her use of Shakespeare, Miss Cather has, without violating the consistency of her narrative method, given the reader an opportunity to bypass Nellie and see into the mind of Myra herself."[20] Nellie tells us that Myra "used to lie back and repeat the old ones she knew by heart, the long declamations from *Richard II* or *King John*"(83). In *Richard II*, the imprisoned king comes to recognize his own guilt and responsibility, rediscovers courage and pride, and dies with an aspiring spirit. *King John* develops through a series of contrasts between the king himself and the characters surrounding him so that, at the end, he seems no more than one small element in the confusion of events. The word "headlands," however, is mentioned three times in the last pages of the novel, and, because Myra chooses to call the headland "Gloucester's cliff," we must deal with *King Lear*. It is possible to propose that Myra knowingly dares fate, hoping to cheat death as Gloucester does when he throws himself off the "cliff" and awakens to find himself alive. Myra loses because Nellie opts to let her have her headstrong way, ultimately allowing her to commit suicide through the foolhardy act of spending the night on the exposed cliff in her weakened and fragile state.[21]

Here, as in *A Lost Lady*, Cather uses imagery to expand her reader's understanding of the characters; in this novel it is especially significant because there is so little description or reflection. Animal imagery tips us off to Myra's predatory and passionate nature: her hair looks like "the fleece of a Persian goat or some animal that bore silky fur" (6). Myra is "swathed in furs" (20) when she meets Lydia and Nellie at the train station; after she has left Oswald, she wears a fur hat (53). Myra's mouth "seemed to curl and twist about like a little snake" (54); she refers to herself and Oswald as being "safely hidden—in earth, like a pair of old foxes!" (61–62). No detail is wasted. Myra wears carved amethysts (6), which are purple—the color of royalty and passion like the violet flowers, the violet evening, the purple drapes, and the ink with which Oswald inscribed the book of poetry—and which eventually become Nellie's chilling adornment. Amethysts have the power to prevent nightmares, but they are also a talisman against intoxication. Nellie can never see the "bright beginning of a love story" (104), that intoxication of love, without hearing Myra cry out against her mortal enemy.

Oswald's "winey-yellow" topazes suggest the Dionysian-Apollonian split in his personality:[22] symbol of his duplicity and infidelity to Myra, they appear again in juxtaposition to the young female journalist with whom he dines during Myra's last illness. Ewan Gray's choice of opals for Esther meets with disapproval from Myra: "Love itself draws on a woman nearly all the bad luck in the world; why, for mercy's sake, add opals?" (28). Does she then believe that the source of a woman's bad luck in love is, in fact, her lover? Recognition of these commonly accepted symbols and metaphors increases the reader's accessibility to the story that remains untold but is intuited. Wilber Urban explains that Cather instinctively knows:

> The *vis poetics* of language, out of which conscious poetry develops, consists in its power to evoke images, but images are the means of intuition, not the intuition itself; the intuition is bound up with imagination and imagery but . . . is not identical with it.[23]

The tone of voice a reader hears when Myra says, "It's disgusting in a man to lie for personal decorations. A woman might do it, now, . . . for pearls!" (54) has a lot to do with his or her reaction to the word "pearls."

In this novel, as in *A Lost Lady*, with which it has so frequently been compared, Cather again uses the aural image of a woman's laugh to demonstrate her characteristic manner. Cather uses the image here, however, to denote another kind of woman; Myra is certainly no Daisy prototype. In the very first chapter, Nellie tells us:

> Mrs. Henshawe seemed to remember all the old stories and the old jokes that had been asleep for twenty years.
>
> "How good it is," my mother explained, "to hear Myra laugh again!"
>
> Yes, it was good. It was sometimes terrible, too, as I was to find out later. She had an angry laugh, for instance, that I still shiver to remember. Any stupidity made Myra laugh—I was destined to hear that one very often! Untoward circumstances, accidents, even disasters, provoked her mirth. And it was always mirth, not hysteria; there was a spark of zest and wild humour in it. (10)

Myra does not laugh in kindness or delight or joy, and when

Nellie meets the Henshawes ten years later, we should be alert, for she finds unchanged that "old gay laugh" (61).

For Susan Rosowski, *My Mortal Enemy* is Nellie's novel, which has as its heart her "expanding narrative consciousness"; she points out that "changes in consciousness accompany changes in narrative structure, as the woman Myra questions the romantic myth of which she has been a part."[24] One of the most interesting experiments in this book is Cather's use of Nellie as narrator. Because we have established earlier that the choice of a point of view is essential to the novelist's manipulation of his or her reader, we must consider what the choice of first-person narration in *My Mortal Enemy* accomplishes. Wayne C. Booth has suggested that narrators fall into three categories: implied authors, who are actually authors' "second selves"; undramatized narrators, who participate little in the events of the story; and dramatized narrators, who are neither narrator-agents, reflecting on the action of the plot, or observers, recording the action as they see it unfolding.[25] We might be tempted to relegate Nellie Birdseye to the ranks of observing narrators, except that to do so ignores the insistence on the "I" of the narrating voice and also begs the question of Nellie's reliability. With Nellie, Cather creates several viewpoints within one center of consciousness, constructing a multiple viewpoint point of view in the first-person as she did in the third-person narration of *A Lost Lady*. The effect is that we see Myra, as we see Marian, from many angles, but here the use of first person deliberately intensifies our identification with Nellie as we see Myra through her eyes.

In this book, Nellie has three voices: her adult voice, which is the actual narrating voice and which I call the forty-five-year-old voice; her young voice, which is her twenty-five-year-old voice; and her childhood voice, which is her fifteen-year-old voice. We also have access to Nellie's memories, because we particpate in her consciousness, and therefore, we can experience Nellie as a six-year-old child, Lydia as a young woman, and even, through those old family stories, Myra as a twenty-year old woman. By shifting from one voice to another, Cather creates those juxtapositions that allow for reader distancing and irony while preserving the unity of narration necessary in such an unfurnished work. The distancing that is possible with third-person narration is accomplished because a vacuole exists between voices in which the reader appreciates the irony of the situation. The adult Nellie passes no judgment, although she recounts the scene, and the reader fills the void. Signals to these shifts are the names by which Nellie calls the other characters. The child Nellie calls Myra Mrs. Henshawe, Mrs. Myra, or Myra Driscoll, if she's entertaining fairy-tale notions about her; when Nellie is speaking in her adult voices, either at age twenty-five or forty-five, she uses Myra. Oswald is Mr. Henshawe to the child, but Oswald when the older Nellie reflects on him.[26] In the passage we considered earlier, we can examine this technique as Cather shifts from the fifteen-year-old child to the adult. Young Nellie comments on Mrs. Henshawe's ability to remember the old stories, but adult Nellie reflects on the terrible effect of that laughter, indicting that she had been the victim of it often. Here the reader is involved because this kind of shift necessitates an evaluation, an assessment of what is actually going on. The child reports innocently, the adult suggests consequences, and the reader draws conclusions.

Just as she does in *The Professor's House*, Cather experiments with time in *My Mortal Enemy*. James Schroeter has also mentioned this point in comparing the book to Edith Wharton's *Ethan Frome*. He says:

> Like *Ethan Frome*, it embodies a theme, a story and a chronological span that would, if developed according to normal novelistic technique, make for a longer than average novel. Instead the book is pared ruthlessly to the bone.
>
> But whereas *Ethan Frome* makes a completed picture, rather like a long short story, *My Mortal Enemy* reaches outside the canvas.[27]

Here Cather concerns herself with the problem of compressing a period of indefinite time into two points in time ten years apart so that the story will reach beyond the page and enlist the reader's imagination in its final and completed effect. The events Nellie recounts, and that we can assign to the fictional time of the novel, occur when she is fifteen and twenty-five; she is very specific about that information in the opening sentences of parts 1 and 2: "I first met Myra Henshawe when I was fifteen" (1); "Ten years after that visit to New York I happened to be in a sprawling overgrown Westcoast city" (58).

Nellie is speaking from some point in time after the story is concluded, however, and we are led into this present time by the present tense of the last section: "I still have the string of amethysts, but they are unlucky. If I take them out of their box and wear them, I feel all evening a chill over my heart" (104). Because we have access to Nellie's memories, Cather can also extend the time of the novel in the other direction, even into a time that is before Nellie's birth. The fairy-tale tone and references of these sections of memory and old family stories suggest eternal time. Readers know that fairy tales took place a long time ago, in a land far away. Using this frame of reference also gives Cather's tale an association beyond historical time; these characters have universal meaning, and their actions universal application, just as those mythic stories of love and hate demonstrate human nature's deepest desires and resolutions.

Having established several voices for her narrator and a broad sweep of time that must impinge on the brief space of the book's action, Cather arranges her facts and manipulates the manner in which we receive them to elicit an intense emotional response. By juxtaposing Nellie's different voices, she creates vacuoles that invite the reader to create a unity that covers many more years than are numbered in the book and many more relationships than are divulged. Referring in to such vacuoles and using his own term *blank*, Wolfgang Iser explains the mechanics of this phenomenon:

> In this sense, they (blanks) function as a self-regulating structure in communication; what they suspend turns into a propellant for the reader's imagination, making him supply what has been withheld. Thus the self-regulating structure operates according to the principle of homeostasis. As we have seen, the balance may be weighted in many different ways, but the structure itself remains constant: it is an empty space which provokes and guides the ideational activity. In this respect, it is a basic element of the interaction between text and reader.[28]

In the brief six pages of chapter 6, part 1, Nellie's voice changes ten times. She overhears the *Henshawes'* quarreling; remarks on *Oswald's* "distinctly malicious chuckle" (50); reflects from her adult vantage point that "What I felt was fear" (52); and has lunch with *Oswald*, during which she remarks from her present vantage point: "I have since seen those half-moon eyes in other people, and they were always inscrutable; fronted the world with courtesy and kindness, but one never got behind them" (52). Fifteen-year-old Nellie determines that "I should never like Mrs. *Myra* so well again" (52). Nellie and her Aunt Lydia prepare to leave New York without seeing the *Henshawes*, because *Myra* has sent a note saying her friend is ill, but when they get settled on the train *Myra Henshawe* arrives, having left her husband.

The child Nellie reports that "All day *Mrs. Myra* was jolly and agreeable" (53), but when they arrive in Pittsburgh, the porter takes *Myra's* luggage, and the adult Nellie notices her "icy little smile" (54).[29] The chapter ends with the child's voice: "Aunt Lydia was very angry. 'I'm sick of Myra's dramatics,' she declared. 'I've done with them. A man never *is* justified, but if ever a man was . . .'" (54). The reader is left at the end of the chapter to appreciate the irony of the situation: Oswald has been unfaithful; Myra is angry with Lydia and Oswald; and Nellie is confused and upset by behavior only her adult self will come to understand. The reader fills the vacuoles, supplies the unity, and understands all that has been suppressed and cut away.

My Mortal Enemy is a brilliant technical success. In the book, Cather practices all the methods she has developed to simplify and cut away all excess detail, and yet she makes clear to the reader all that is not recorded on the page. The events of *My Mortal Enemy* come to mind easily and with a cinemagraphic clarity; its characters linger in the imagination with a surprising complexity. Critics have wondered why Cather wrote only this one novel *démeublé*, why the tone and technique in her next novel changed. It seems possible that the writing of this book was an exercise in compression, more an intellectual challenge than an artistic re-creation of the teasing memory. After *My Mortal Enemy*, she had no need to write another unfurnished novel because in this brief work she had finally demonstrated that her principle of the unfurnished novel actually worked in practice as she maintained in theory. Working strictest boundaries and using the most refined techniques, Willa Cather managed to write the novel *démeublé* in her own clear style.

Conclusion

Willa Cather left an unpublished fragment that was included in *On Writing* as "Light on Adobe Walls." In it she writes:

> Art is a concrete and personal and rather childish thing after all—no matter what people do to graft it into science and make it socio-logical and psychological; it is not good at all unless it is let alone to be itself—a game of make-believe, of re-production, very exciting and delightful to people who have an ear for it or an eye for it. Art is too terribly human to be very "great," perhaps.[1]

Howard N. Doughty, Jr., "disputes the fundamental point" here,[2] and suggests that Cather could not seriously entertain an idea that diminishes the "greatness" of art. It seems more consistent, however, to propose that this statement instead embodies all that Cather believes about the creation of art. We have seen that, to Cather, art is an occasion for a personal creation, provided by a writer for a reader; each must share in the emotional experi-ence of the work for it to be successful. For the work itself to be successful art, the effect of that experience must linger in the consciousness of each long after the story is done.

In "Miss Jewett," Cather relates the lesson Sarah Orne Jewett taught her about the process of creation:

> when a writer makes anything that belongs to Literature . . . his mate-rial goes through a process very different from that by which he merely makes a good story. No one can define this process exactly; but certainly persistence, survival, recurrence in the writer's mind, are highly characteristic of it. The shapes and scenes that have "teased" the mind for years, when they do at last get themselves rightly put down, make a much higher order of writing, and a much more costly, than the most vivid and vigorous transfer of immediate impressions.[3]

Cather's long apprenticeship gave her the equipment and the perspective she needed to translate mere experience into art.

David Daiches remarks that "it was a good sign that Miss Cather began her career as a novelist by demonstrating an interest in the craft of fiction rather than by slapping on to paper her more autobiographical impulses."[4] She never really developed the language that would explain just how that could be done, however, and her description of the creative process here is just as ephemeral as any of her critical statements.

The style that results from this creative process also defies analysis, but we have seen that the techniques which produce it can be enumerated. Simplicity and compression mark the Catherian work of art, and these are achieved by the concrete detail, the suggestive word, and their juxtaposition in a form so inevitable that "the design is the story and the story is the design."[5] In *Symbol and Metaphor in Human Experience*, Martin Foss explains:

> Meaning lies beyond words, the one as well as the combination of the many. It grows out of the communion of concepts, uses and disposes of the words according to its own insight, in a tension of the present in which no single word stands out, but is lost in the process and its structure of articulation. . . . In true poetry the complex rituals are turned into simplicity of meaning, for meaning is simple when expressive, and poetry had to achieve this simplicity in order to overcome the complex mechanism of its art and structure.[6]

Cather also believed that meaning exists beyond the words, and that, however complex the technical structure of her work, the style itself must be simple, clear, and beautifully smooth. The direction of her work from the early reviews and columns to the final experiment of *Sapphira and the Slave Girl* demonstrates this principle. The first book that Cather published was *April Twilights* (1903), a collection of poems. Later, she described the creation of art as that "sudden inner explosion and enlightenment,"[7] which she had previously experienced only in the conception of poetry before she found her way in fiction with the design of *O Pioneers!* John Randall writes: "I soon discovered that she wrote a prose so poetic as to demand extensive imagistic analysis before I could even begin to determine what her ideas were like."[8] David Massey says: "Because she uses such compressed language . . . Cather invites the attention to detail that we give to poetry."[9] Indeed, if we talk about imagery, compression, suggestiveness, and emotional response, it seems as though the standards of poetry apply better to Cather's work than any others. We might also remember that Elizabeth Sergeant, who knew Cather well during those years between 1922 and 1926 (the years of *A Lost Lady, The Professor's House,* and *My Mortal Enemy*), recalls her friend's own reflections on these works:

> She said, still, that her novels were transcriptions of love for people and places. But now form seemed to assume greater significance. Her aim was to create a work of art out of subject matter, new or old, that had "teased" her, and had left, as she said, a deep impression upon her. Mind and invention were not her tools; the decisive element was intuitive, poetical, almost mystical perception.[10]

Ezra Pound says: "Great literature is simple language charged with meaning to the utmost possible degree."[11] Like the modernists with whom she is not identified, like the imagists and "free verse bunch from the Middle West"[12] whom she did not like, Cather forged her own way in great literature by understanding this very principle. Freed by her belief that idea would dictate form, and confident that the sensitive reader would respond to both, she allowed herself to test the boundaries that defined art.

Willa Cather wrote twelve novels, and each of them is a complex work that integrates content and form in a different experiment. From the beginning, Cather maintained that feeling is the true criteria of art. As early as 1895, she wrote: "To feel greatly is genius and to make others feel is art."[13] All of the works have as their purpose, then, the evocation of a response in the reader. In this study, we have examined those techniques that Cather developed to evoke the emotional response of her reader—that intuitive, sensitive, nonjudgmental, and imaginative reader who could bring his or her own analogy-forming desire to order a puzzling universe to the work of art. To this end, she manipulates the few details of her stories in the most effective juxtapositions, producing those reader-involving vacuoles that she knew all about long before they were defined as blanks, negations, lacunae of indeterminacy, or indeterminate areas in imagination by the recent reader-response critics.

Eudora Welty says, "My own feeling is that along with her other superior gifts Willa Cather had a rare sureness as to her subject matter, the knowledge of just what to touch and what not to touch in the best interests of the story."[14] This sureness of touch—the ability to know what should be left in and, more important, what left out—and her confidence in the reaction it will produce can be attributed to both the intensity with which

Cather remembered scene and detail and her ability to look at experience with a "childish" eye, which not only sees beyond the surface facts of reality but also feels the effect of that sight. To feel, one must in some emotional sense participate in an event. Then one must try to make sense of what still puzzles one after the eyes are averted. Participation is necessary for intense feeling. To assure the intensity, Cather forces her reader to participate with the alert attention and puzzlement of a child. Cather's description of art as "childish" therefore cuts two ways: her writing demonstrates the simplicity we associate with childish things and it also requires a childlike, intuitive, and receptive sensibility to appreciate it, with ultimate judgment withheld until the work is perceived as a whole.

Characteristic of Cather's work is her use of sensual imagery. As she once said, "Art is a matter of enjoyment through the five senses."[15] Richard Giannone and Joseph X. Brennen have contributed substantially to our understanding of Cather's aural metaphors and references;[16] we also must recognize her ability to make the reader "see" the story. As Welty tells us:

> Willa Cather would like our minds to receive what she is showing us not by its description—however beautiful—but as the thing described, the living thing itself. To this end she may eliminate its picture, the better to make us see something really there.[17]

To make her readers see, Cather adopts cinemagraphic techniques that encourage visualization, which again suggests her similarities to the modernists. Lillian and Edward Bloom have observed:

> By capturing within a single novel a series of "great moments," each paradoxically trivial, she was—if we may borrow a Joycean image— recreating life out of life and was writing by her own terms and definition a realistic novel. Her vision of life, whether for the individual or his social group, was a series of pictures . . . to be caught by the "camera's eye" or mind.[18]

Willa Cather's radical nature, expressed outwardly in her years of adolescent rebellion, found new ways of reproducing life in art through new ideas derived from the original possibilities she suggested, from new forms made by the rearrangement of familiar objects, and from new uses of old forms. Her use of immigrants as serious characters in a serious novel was avant-garde in 1913, and, although her experiments in form have not drawn as much attention, they prove to be as complex as anything Proust, Joyce, Gide, or Robbe-Grillet has done. Their chief characteristic is what they show as truly necessary for literary life, and what is demonstrably expendable.

As we have seen, Willa Cather's designs rely as much on what has been left out as on those elements of juxtaposition or details of plot that have been left in. In the past it has been difficult to discuss the effect of these gaps on the reader, although their effect has been observed, because we have not had critical language that aptly describes something that is not there. Therefore, I have proposed that we borrow from science the term *vacuole* to demonstrate the significant absences in Cather's texts.

Cather's use of vacuoles is a natural outgrowth of her bifocal modern vision that perceives life in terms of juxtaposition, and we find vacuoles throughout the work. As we have seen, Cather uses vacuoles as signals for voice changes, plot advancement, character amplification, mood shifts, and emotional impact. In chapter 3 we have seen that Willa Cather instinctively uses these vacuoles from her earliest novel. We find gaps of information and juxtaposition of detail even in *Alexander's Bridge*, which is clearly derivative and about which Cather wrote to Fanny Butcher: "In this case, my interest in the reviewer has outlived my interest in the novel, for I don't think much of that book now."[19] As we have noted, however, it is in writing *O Pioneers!* that she actually understands the relationship between content and form, between artistic vision and juxtaposition. She once said: "The thing worth while is always unplanned. Any art that is a result of preconcerted plans is a dead baby."[20] For her, the explosion of understanding that came with the juxtaposition of the two stories that make up the novel is the exact effect she means to create with each succeeding work of art. David Daiches points out that she does not achieve completely successful unity in the book, but that its vitality and strength overcome this deficiency. He says: "Episodic and unevenly patterned as it is, *O Pioneers!* has nevertheless moments of strange force and beauty and a general air of power and assurance which are remarkable enough and proclaim a significant talent."[21] Although the vacuoles are structuring elements in this book, and although they are certainly responsible for that vitality and strength to which the reader is compelled to respond because he or she must supply continuation, Cather is still learning the potential of the vacuole here and we do not find that tight structure which she is able to achieve in *A Lost Lady*.

As we have seen earlier, *The Song of the Lark* represents an experiment in which Cather tells everything, and through which she learns that her memories are best served by a strict process of selectivity. Although we cannot demonstrate the vacuole easily with this book, gaps are here because Cather sees everything in juxtaposition to something else. In fact, in her dissertation, Jean Lavon Throckmorton points out that Cather revised her material to emphasize the gaps:

> In the revised version of *The Song of the Lark*, the last pages of Part VI, "Kronborg," and the first pages of the Epilogue are structurally connected by a clear juxtaposition of focus on Spanish Johnny and Tillie Kronborg, respectively. This juxtaposition, after Cather's revision, binds the sections together like two funnels placed end to end, forming the shape of an hourglass.[22]

This juxtaposition also necessitates a vacuole in which the reader can understand the significance of these two characters for Thea. In this story, however, Cather primarily chooses to explain rather than suggest, and she expects the reader to respond to the vast accumulation of detail. Although we can learn a great deal about Cather, the person, from *The Song of the Lark*—given the autobiographical elements—it is perhaps the most atypical of the style we are investigating in this study.[23] From this book, we learn that the artist Willa Cather was not unwilling to set unfamiliar limitations for each work, that each did represent a new effort to get her conceptions down on paper, and that she approached each with an openness to the requirements of the material at hand.

If we use her own criteria, then Willa Cather's *My Ántonia* succeeds as a work of art; most criticism focuses on its power to evoke an emotional response. In fact, James Woodress remarks: "Even a hardened reader finishes this novel choked up with emotions. How, one wonders, does Willa Cather manage it?"[24] James E. Miller suggests that "we sense what we cannot detect—structural elements subtly at work reinforcing and sharpening the aroused feeling."[25] The undetectable elements are the vacuoles; the very presence of inset narrative necessitates gaps to which the reader must respond. Although Cather maintains a balance here between vacuole and detail that reminds one of poetic compression, the richness of imagery and the scope of the novel make Cather's use of vacuole less obvious in this work than in the later books. Thus, the reader is caught up in the story more through associative imagery, point of view, and a cyclic sense of time rather than through the necessity to fill the vacuole.

We noted earlier that when Cather wrote *One of Ours* she cut out all descriptive work, because her redheaded prairie boy did not "see pictures."[26] In this book, Cather uses vacuoles in place of description, and the amount of frustration expressed in the criticism should indicate how successful she was at reproducing Claude's frustration in the reader. Frederick Griffiths calls Claude, Cather's "hero *démeublé*," explaining that his rough simple outlines resulted from the process of simplification.[27]

Writing an essay in which she attempts to define what she expects art to do clarified for Cather the kind of fiction she wanted to write. In the process of writing the next three novels—*A Lost Lady*, *The Professor's House*, and *My Mortal Enemy*—she achieves artistic autonomy, works out the practices that best produce reader response, and actually produces her unfurnished novel. In the books that we have considered, Willa Cather realizes the possibilities of reader manipulation by drawing on a common fund of knowledge, by experimenting with narrative point of view, by intensely visualizing scenes and episodes, and, finally, by exploring the power of the vacuole created by her use of juxtaposition. In these novels, Cather concentrates on those techniques that produce the greatest possible reader response, particularly the vacuole, because it allows her to suppress and cut away while demanding the reader's utmost attention. Having written a work in which the vacuoles are integral to both the structure and meaning of the story, and in which the reader must actively cooperate to achieve that emotional catharsis, Cather turns to explorations of tone, mood, and the limits of conventional generic expectations in the books following *My Mortal Enemy*. The use of vacuoles as a means of suggestiveness and reader manipulation is a technique that appears with such consummate ease in the last four novels that it is apparent it has become part of Cather's method of organization, part of her vision of the world, an essential element of that style which she perfected through the writing of *A Lost Lady*, *The Professor's House*, and *My Mortal Enemy*.

Once we have developed the critical language to address the void in Willa Cather's work, and once we demonstrate the development of that technique and her use of the void in the process of reader response, it becomes merely repetitious to point out instances where vacuoles exist in Cather's other works. Therefore, we will briefly review just some of the uses of vacuoles in the last four novels to illustrate Cather's masterful dexterity in handling those essential absences that her style, sensibility, and artistic intention demand.

In an interesting and telling comment to Fanny Butcher, Cather describes the writing of *Death Comes for the Archbishop*. She says, "It's an altogether new kind for me, and how I loved doing it. It was as if you had, after playing only modern composers, taken the time and used the control to practice Bach awhile without any comparison,"[28] substantiating our suggestion that the writing of *My Mortal Enemy* proved to Cather her own technical skill and released her to apply that expertise to still different artistic challenges.

Cather stated that she wanted to write something in the style of a legend when she wrote *Archbishop*. The use of vacuoles in this novel underlines this intent and demonstrates the exquisite control that she developed in handling both the detail and the void. Josephine Jessup finds a greater concentration of style in this book than in any preceding it and suggests that its structural looseness puts it almost outside the genre of novel.[29] Here the accents are always on the unexpected; the expected occurs in the vacuole but in one so understated as to be almost unremarked. The reader is impelled to create the story of the missionaries' lives from the ordered details and disjointed episodes that make up the text of the work. As James Woodress observes:

> Below its smooth face . . . the novel resonates wth allegory, symbol, and allusion. Form still follows function in the organization, but the structure required this time to write a modern saint's life was far more complex than the structures she had used before. Previously causal relationships connected events in her novels, but here she made no attempt to explain how or why things happened. Events are narrated without being related to causes or linked to results, and things have importance in relation to their religious significance. This is Cather's most elaborately contrived fiction and invites comparison with the allusiveness and technical virtuosity of other major twentieth-century modernist works.[30]

Shadows on the Rock is an experiment in tone, and this consideration must take precedence over all others when we discuss it. Again, Cather's use of vacuoles underlines her primary objective to create a work in which mood guarantees a unity of effect and consistency of impression. The vacuoles here exist to maintain a leisurely pacing of the story, and to emphasize the emotional and physical distance between the wilderness and civilization.

We have already seen that *Lucy Gayheart* uses cinemagraphic techniques that rely to a certain extent on a deft handling of both the significant telling detail and the vacuole to involve the reader. In addition, we have mentioned the reversal of reader expectations in *Sapphira and the Slave Girl*, which also provides vacuoles and consequent reader response as it deals with Southern conventions, the woman as role player, doubleness, and time shifting. In these last four novels, Cather's use of vacuole has become as natural to her as her use of color, strong verbs, figurative language, and economy—all technical elements contributing to an undefinable style that is the artist's own manner of recording, re-creating, and sharing experience.

Bernice Slote points out that "from the beginning Willa Cather joined art and religion, not only in the allegorical kingdom of art but in her primary belief that man's creation shares in some divine power."[31] Divine power creates life. To share in that divine power and to create the work of art, however, writers must devote themselves entirely to that production. In the novels, the materials of the everyday—the dust—receive the breath of life from the novelist's disciplined technique, her art. Those then-pulsating forms are juxtaposed with a self-consciousness that befits a modernist. Cather never loses sight of the work of art as the made thing, a creation that does not reproduce random or meaningless life, but that reproduces the effect of life, thereby re-creating the emotional experience of life. Just as the novels evolve from Cather's memories, they also evolve from her modernist attitude toward art. We find that they comment explicitly on the relationship between art and reality even as we participate in the construction of a fiction.

Frank Lentricchia stresses the significance of the void in the creation of artistic reality, which recent literary criticism has begun to address:

> The very best that self-consciousness can do is point to the empty space, the nothingness stretching out endlessly in "front" of fiction. It cannot say where that empty space becomes filled with something called reality—something which would not be mediated by fiction, or consciousness, or self-consciousness. It can only tell us that fictive discourse may not traverse that space.[32]

In this study, we have seen what Willa Cather has done with the emptiness. Fictive discourse itself cannot traverse that space, the nothingness between the reader and text. Sculpted fictions can, however, by inviting the reader to the creation of a reality that cannot be divined by the ear, nor found on the page. Willa Cather's fictions are meant for the reader who can bring to them imagination enough to understand and fill that final vacuole.

Notes

Preface

1. Willa Cather, "Miss Jewett," in *Not Under Forty* (New York: Alfred A. Knopf, 1964), 78–9.
2. Recent criticism has just begun to address the nature of Cather's modernism. James Woodress briefly discusses Cather's modernism in *Willa Cather: A Literary Life* (Lincoln: University of Nebraska Press, 1987). In *The Voyage Perilous: Willa Cather's Romanticism* (Lincoln: University of Nebraska Press, 1986), Susan Rosowski points out modernist themes in *The Professor's House, Shadows on the Rock,* and *Sapphira and the Slave Girl.* Cather has been compared to Georgia O'Keefe by Jack Collins in "The Literary Endeavor of Willa Cather (As Inspired by Joan Crane's Bibliography)," *Willa Cather Pioneer Memorial Newsletter* 32 (Fall 1988): 33–37. Only Phyllis Rose, however, ("Modernism: The Case of Willa Cather," in *Modernism Reconsidered,* ed. Robert Keily and John Hildebidle [Cambridge: Harvard University Press, 1983], 123–45), has actually made a case for Cather as a modernist. Rose bases her well-delivered argument on Cather's "modernist urge to simplify and to suggest the eternal through the particular" (124). Using analogies to the work of Cézanne, Picasso, Matisse, O'Keefe, and Pollack, among others, Rose defends Cather's modern attitude, and demonstrates her particular version of modernism seen in her use of the monumental landscape and primitive cultures of the American Southwest, her use of inset narrative, and her stringent simplification of both character and style.
3. Wolfgang Iser, *The Act of Reading* (London: Routledge & Kegan Paul, 1979), 34.
4. Edith Lewis, *Willa Cather Living* (New York: Alfred A. Knopf, 1953), 17.

Introduction

1. Katherine Anne Porter, "The Calm, Pure Art of Willa Cather," *New York Times Book Review,* 25 September 1949, 1.
2. Bernice Slote, "Willa Cather," in *Sixteen Modern American Writers,* ed. Jackson R. Bryer (Durham, N.C.: Duke University Press, 1974), 39.
3. George William Greene, "Willa Cather at Mid-Century," *Thought* 32 (Winter 1958): 578.
4. Edward Wagenknecht, *Cavalcade of the American Novel* (New York: Holt, Rinehart and Winston, 1952), 319.
5. Critical interest in Cather has increased in the thirteen years since Slote's assessment; in *American Literary Scholarship 1982,* ed. J. Albert Robbins (Durham, N.C.: Duke University Press, 1984), John J. Murphy points out that the circle of Cather scholars is widening: "Besides broad cultural approaches to the

fiction, activity in Cather's case divides according to two interests: studies primarily devoted to the woman herself—her sexual preferences, childhood, etc.—and studies attempting to analyze the technique of the fiction within world and American literary contexts" (223). The publication of Phyllis Robinson's *Willa: The Life of Willa Cather* (Garden City, N.Y.: Doubleday) in 1983 and Sharon O'Brien's *Willa Cather: The Emerging Voice* (New York: Oxford University Press) in 1986, both of whom openly consider Cather in terms of her sexual orientation and its relation to the work, indicates that Cather herself is still more fascinating to some than her technical contributions to the craft of fiction. Woodress's detailed and definitive biography, *Literary Life*, supersedes all previous biographies, provides a fine critical introduction to Cather's work, and is of inestimable worth to scholars.

6. John Barth, "A Few Words About Minimalism," *New York Times Book Review*, 28 December 1986, 1–2, 15. Barth writes: "'And don't tell a word more than you absolutely need to,' added the young Ernest Hemingway, who thus described his 'new Theory' in the early 1920s: 'You could omit anything if you knew what you omitted, and the omitted part would strengthen the story and make people feel more than they understood'" (2). It is particularly exasperating that Hemingway refused to acknowledge any debt at all to Cather for his "iceberg theory" and furthermore actually disparaged her talent. Fitzgerald, on the other hand, engaged in correspondence with the older writer and willingly conceded that he had learned a great deal about technique from her. A discussion of this can be found in greater depth in James E. Miller, *F. Scott Fitzgerald: His Art and His Technique* (New York: New York University Press, 1964).

7. Reynolds Price, "Men Creating Woman," *New York Times Book Review*, 9 November 1986, 1, 16, 18, 20.

8. Merrill Maguire Skaggs, "Willa Cather's Experimental Southern Novel," *Mississippi Quarterly* 34 (Winter 1981): 3.

Chapter 1. The Mystery of Style

1. Richard Ohmann, "Generative Grammars and the Concept of Literary Style," in *Linguistics and Literary Style*, ed. Donald C. Freeman (New York: Holt, Rinehart and Winston, 1970), 259.

2. Merrill Maguire Skaggs, "Poe's Shadow on *Alexander's Bridge*," *Mississippi Quarterly* 35 (Fall 1982): 365–74.

3. The exception is *The Song of the Lark*, in which, Cather tells us, she tried "the full-blooded method, which told everything about everybody" (Willa Cather, "My First Novels [There Were Two]," in *On Writing* [New York: Alfred A. Knopf, 1953], 96). She continues by pointing out that this method was not congenial to her. It is interesting for our study that she "experimented" with the method before rejecting it altogether.

4. Harlan Hatcher, *Creating the Modern American Novel* (New York: Russell & Russell, 1965), 59.

5. Philip Gerber, *Willa Cather* (Boston: Twayne Publishers, 1975), 161.

6. Marion Marsh Brown and Ruth Crone, *Willa Cather: The Woman and Her Works* (New York: Charles Scribner's Sons, 1970), 152.

7. In his preface to *The Patterns of Literary Style* (University Park: Pennsylvania State University Press, 1971), Joseph P. Strelka reminds us of the varieties of definitions that try to pin down the exact meaning of style: Saint-Beuve's

comment that the only thing immortal in literature is style; F. W. Bateson's statement that style is nearer the working of the creative imagination than linguistics; Buffon's famous contention that *"Le style c'est l'homme même"* (1). He also points out the further complication that style can mean the particular characteristics of a genre, epoch, or literary art in general as well as the peculiar characteristics of any given writer. We should limit our discussion, however, to those definitions that might shed light on our understanding of Willa Cather's personal style, noting that we have set such limits. All of these definitions acknowledge style as the essential expression of the artist's personal creativity; none of these is sufficient to secure a solid grasp of the essential Cather. Webster provides the following definitions of style: "manner or mode of expression in language; way of putting thoughts into words . . . specific or characteristic manner of expression, execution, construction, or design, in any art period, work, employment, etc. . . . distinction, excellence, originality, and character in any form of artistic or literary expression . . . the way in which anything is made or done; manner" ("Style," in *Webster's New World Dictionary of the American Language* [Cleveland: World, 1960], 1449).

8. Willa Cather, "Katherine Mansfield," in *Forty*, 134–35.

9. William Curtin, "Willa Cather: Individualism and Style," *Colby Library Quarterly* 8 (June 1968): 37.

10. I. A. Richards, *Poetries and Sciences*, a reissue of *Science and Poetry* (New York: W. W. Norton, 1970), 44.

11. Latrobe Carroll, "Willa Sibert Cather," in *Willa Cather in Person*, ed. L. Brent Bohlke (Lincoln: University of Nebraska Press, 1986), 20.

12. Cather, "Jewett," in *Forty*, 80.

13. Cather, "On *Shadows*," in *Writing*, 15.

14. Woodress, *A Literary Life*, 254.

15. Richards, *Poetries*, 44.

16. For the basic biographical material, a good introduction to Willa Cather can be found in Mildred R. Bennett, *The World of Willa Cather* (Lincoln: University of Nebraska Press, 1961); E. K. Brown, *Willa Cather: A Critical Biography* (New York: Alfred A. Knopf, 1953); David Daiches, *Willa Cather: A Critical Introduction* (Westport, Conn.: Greenwood Press, 1957). Woodress offers a comprehensive biography in *Literary Life*. Personal recollections of Cather can be found in Edith Lewis, *Willa Cather Living: A Personal Record* (New York: Alfred A. Knopf, 1953); and Elizabeth Shepley Sergeant, *Willa Cather: A Memoir* (Philadelphia: J. B. Lippincott, 1953). Two studies have discussed Cather's life in terms of her sexual orientation: Robinson, *Life of Cather*, is a full-length biography; and O'Brien, *Emerging Voice*, is a study of Cather's early years. Two excellent scholarly works make Cather's early work available to us: *The World and the Parish*, ed. William Curtin (Lincoln: University of Nebraska Press, 1970); and *The Kingdom of Art: Willa Cather's First Principles and Critical Statements 1893–1896*, ed. Bernice Slote (Lincoln: University of Nebraska Press, 1967). Cather's interviews, speeches, and ten published letters are collected in Bohlke, *Cather in Person*. Many other excellent critical works deal with Cather's biography in terms of a particular aspect of the work.

17. Slote, *Kingdom of Art*, 31.

18. Cather, "Jewett," in *Forty*, 76.

19. Cather, "Mansfield," in *Forty*, 144.

20. Mildred Bennett, "Introduction," in Willa Cather, *Collected Short Fiction* (Lincoln: University of Nebraska Press, 1969), xvii.

21. Cather, "Review of *Our Flat*," *Nebraska State Journal*, 8 March 1896, in Slote, *Kingdom of Art*, 68–96. Because Willa Cather's years of journalism contributed to her growth as a stylist, and because Ernest Hemingway's career as a journalist shaped his style as well, it is worth noting that the limited areas in which their styles are similar might derive from this common element in their backgrounds. Cather's deceptively simple, clean style, built on carefully selected ordinary words and short declarative sentences, is a result of increasingly stringent excision and simplification of the ornate and florid journalistic style that she had employed. Cather was acutely aware of this change in her style, and remembered Charles H. Gere's editorial tolerance fondly in a letter to Will Owen Jones on 22 March 1927: "I was paid one dollar a column—which was certaintly quite all my high-stepping rhetoric was worth. Those outpourings were pretty dreadful but . . . he let me step as high as I wished. It was rather hard on his readers, perhaps, but it was good for me, because it enabled me to riot in fine writing until I got to hate it, and began slowly to recover" (Bohlke, *Cather in Person*, 181). Conversely, Hemingway's minimal style appears to be a result of the transference of a sparser journalistic style (as required on the Kansas City *Star*) to his creative work.

22. Cather, "Art of Fiction," in *Writing*, 102.

23. Gerber, *Cather*, 138.

24. Cather, "The Novel Démeublé," in *Forty*, 48.

25. Cather, "Art of Fiction," in *Writing*, 103.

26. Ibid., 101.

27. Cather, "Jewett," in *Forty*, 81.

28. Dorothy Canfield, quoted in Kathleen D. Byrne and Richard C. Snyder, *Chrysalis: Willa Cather in Pittsburgh 1896–1906* (Pittsburgh: Historical Society of Western Pennsylvania, 1980), 21. Cather's comparison reminds us of a later comparison by Robert Frost of the act of writing poetry with the game of tennis; Cather admired Frost's poetry for its technical brilliance within determined limits.

29. Cather, "A Chance Meeting," *Forty*, 24–25.

30. Willa Cather, interview with Rose C. Feld, "Restlessness Such as Ours Does Not Make For Beauty," *New York Times*, 21 December 1924, in Bohlke, *Cather in Person*, 71.

31. Ibid., 72.

32. Willa Cather, *Shadows on the Rock*, (New York: Alfred A. Knopf, 1959), 25–26.

33. Willa Cather, *Death Comes for the Archbishop* (New York: Vintage, 1971), 39.

34. Granville Hicks, "The Case against Willa Cather," in *Willa Cather and Her Critics*, ed. James Schroeter (Ithaca: Cornell University Press, 1967), 147.

35. Morton Davwen Zabel, *Craft and Character: Texts, Method and Vocation in Modern Fiction* (New York: Viking, 1957), 264–70.

36. We should note here that some of the blame should go to Cather as well. In the prefatory note to *Not Under Forty*, she writes: "The title of this book is meant to be 'arresting' only in the literal sense, like the signs put up for motorists: 'ROAD UNDER REPAIR,' etc. It means that the book will have little interest for people under forty years of age. The world broke in two in 1922 or thereabouts, and the persons and prejudices recalled in these sketches slid back into yesterday's seven thousand years. Thomas Mann, to be sure, belongs immensely to the forward-goers, and they are concerned only with his forward-

ness. But he goes back a long way, and his backwardness is more gratifying to the backward. It is for the backward, and by one of their number, that these sketches were written" (v). Speculation has been focused on 1922, and what precipitated the world's breaking in two; I suggest that attention should be focused on the seven thousand years that make up Cather's "yesterday" to better understand what she meant by the past and why she identified herself as one of the backward. We should also note that 1922 is the year that T. S. Eliot's *The Waste Land*, a new cultural myth that Cather rejected, was published. See also the discussion of *The Professor's House* in chapter 6.

Chapter 2. The Mastery of Technique

1. John H. Randall, *The Landscape and the Looking Glass* (New York: Houghton Mifflin, 1960), x.
2. Mildred Bennett, *My Ántonia: Notes* (Lincoln, Neb.: Cliffs Notes, 1962), 61.
3. Analogies can be made to the creation of art in other areas as well. For instance, the individual tessera in a mosaic is nothing; joined with all the others in a pattern that leaves gaps between the elements, it produces the divine glow that raises the cupola, pavement, or wall to the triumph that endures.
4. Thomas Uzzell, *The Technique of the Novel: A Handbook on the Craft of the Long Narrative* (New York: Citadel Press, 1959), 22.
5. Mark Schorer, "Technique as Discovery" in *The Theory of the Novel*, ed. Philip Stevick (New York: Free Press, 1967), 66.
6. Uzzell, *Technique*, 20.
7. Cather, "Jewett" in *Forty*, 77–78.
8. Ibid., 79–80.
9. Cather, *Kingdom of Art*, 43.
10. Wagenknecht, *American Novel*, 335. In a letter that was published in the *St. Paul Daily News* on 5 March 1922, Cather wrote: "The writer does not 'efface' himself, as you say; he loses himself in the amplitude of his impressions, and in the exciting business of finding all his memories, long-forgotten scenes and faces, running off his pen, as if they were in the ink, and not in his brain at all" (Bohlke, *Cather in Person*, 178).
11. Jean Lavon Throckmorton, "Willa Cather: Artistic Theory and Practice (Volumes 1 and 2)," Ph.D. diss., University of Kansas, 1954, 77. Throckmorton's study is one of several unpublished dissertations that deal with Cather's technique, indicating that, at least on the graduate level of scholarship, a recognized need exists for study in this area. Other interesting and useful sources are David G. Massey, "Simplicity with Suggestiveness in Willa Cather's Revised and Republished Fiction," Ph.D. diss., Drew University, 1979, which considers the revisions that Cather made in terms of the *démeublé* theory; Albert Edward Schmittlein, "Willa Cather's Novels: An Evolving Art," Ph.D. diss., University of Pittsburgh, 1962, which discusses the organic development of the novel and Cather's experiments with time, synthesis, and the tridimensional; and Patricia Lee Yongue, "The Immense Design: A Study of Willa Cather's Creative Process," Ph.D. diss., University of California at Los Angeles, 1972, in which she maintains: "She [Cather] was, in fact, very much a part of her generation of writers who observed and commented on the mainstream of American life and,

quite importantly, upon the course of the country's history. Her literary affiliations, though admittedly with Henry James and Sarah Orne Jewett, were as much with Fitzgerald, Faulkner, Hart Crane, Pound, Eliot and Williams" (14).

12. Cather, "Light on Adobe Walls," in *Writing*, 123.

13. Sergeant, *Memoir*, 133–34.

14. Gabriel Josipovici, *The Lessons of Modernism* (Totowa, N.J.: Rowman & Littlefield, 1977), x.

15. Edward A. and Lillian D. Bloom, *Willa Cather's Gift of Sympathy* (Carbondale: Southern Illinois University Press, 1962), 156–57.

16. Cather came to realize that she could trust herself and her material as a result of writing *O Pioneers!* In a 29 March 1931 interview for the *San Francisco Chronicle*, Cather told Harold Small: "What I write . . . results from a personal explosional experience. All of a sudden, the idea for a story is in my head. It is in the ink bottle when I start to write. But I don't start until the idea has found its own pattern and fixed its proper tone. And it does that; some of the things that I first consider important fade into insignificance, while others that I first glimpse as minor things, grow until they show that they are the important things. It seems a natural process" (Bohlke, *Cather in Person*, 111).

17. Fanny Butcher, *Many Lives—One Love* (New York: Harper & Row, 1972), 358.

18. Wagenknecht, *American Novel*, 335.

19. Daiches, *Cather*, 140, 138.

20. Sergeant, *Memoir*, 200.

21. Curtin, "Individualism and Style," 52.

22. Elizabeth Sergeant, Fanny Butcher, and Dorothy Canfield all have discussed Cather's interest in the contemporary literary scene. We must realize that this does not necessarily mean Cather approved of, or even liked, current trends, nor does it mean that she necessarily disliked everything either, but we must acknowledge that she was aware of the world around her. Susan Rosowski suggests that "she too saw herself as the first of a new literary tradition, yet one which evolved out of the past and from native traditions rather than in revolt against them" (*Voyage Perilous*, 7).

23. O'Brien discusses Cather's avant-garde theories and rebellious behavior during her youth in *Emerging Voice*. She says: "During her college years Cather passed through what she later called her 'Bohemian' phase, a period of unorthodox behavior she ultimately repudiated when she became less interested in opposing convention" (134). Cather's association with the avant-garde at the University of Nebraska gave her a certain mind-set; she liked to consider herself modern, even at that early date. Slote comments: "Was she modern? 'Up-to-date' in matters of general information she certainly was" (*Kingdom of Art*, 33). Sergeant recalls that "in later life, nothing interested her less than what the French call *le movement*, in poetry or novels. The *avant-garde* . . . But in 1913, the story of *le sauvage*, as his mother called him, and above all, his new way of painting, piqued her interest" (*Memoir*, 114). By the time "modern" became new, it was old to Cather.

24. George Schloss, "A Writer's Art," *Hudson Review* 3 (Spring 1950): 153–54.

25. Cather, "Restlessness," in Bohlke, *Cather in Person*, 71.

26. E. K. Brown, "Homage to Willa Cather," *Yale Review* 36 (Autumn 1946): 77.

27. Richard Ellmann and Charles Feidelson, Jr., eds., "Introduction," in *The*

Modern Tradition: Backgrounds of Modern Literature (New York: Oxford University Press, 1965), v.

28. Irving Howe, "The Culture of Modernism," in *Decline of the New* (New York: Harcourt, Brace & World, 1970), 3–4.

29. Josipovici, *Lessons of Modernism*, 109.

30. Harold Fickett and Douglas R. Gilbert, *Flannery O'Connor: Image of Grace* (Grand Rapids, Mich.: William B. Eerdmans, 1986), 1–2.

31. David Craig, *The Real Foundations: Literature and Social Change* (New York: Oxford University Press, 1974), 184.

32. Peter Ackroyd, *Notes For a New Culture: An Essay on Modernism* (New York: Barnes & Noble Books, 1976), 18.

33. Peter Faulkner, *Modernism* (London: Methuen, 1977), 6.

34. Philip Stevick, "The Theory of the Novel" in *Theory of Novel*, 46.

35. "Experiment," in *Webster's New World Dictionary*, 512.

36. Cather, "Jewett," in *Forty*, 80. We might suggest that Cather's belief in literary experimentation began in her youth with her interest in scientific investigation. It is well-known that she was interested in medicine before she chose a literary life, and she defended experimentation in her 1890 high school commencement address, "Superstition versus Investigation": "With the publication of the *Novum Organum* came a revolution in thought; scientists ceased theorizing and began experimenting. . . . It is the most sacred right of man to investigate; we paid dearly for it in Eden; we have been shedding our heart's blood for it ever since. It is ours; we have bought it with a price" (Bohlke, *Cather in Person*, 142). When she turned to the pursuit of art, Cather brought to her endeavor the philosophical equipment for experimentation as well as for absolute dedication to her goal.

37. Lillian D. Bloom with Edward Bloom, "The Poetics of Willa Cather," in *Five Essays on Willa Cather*, ed. John J. Murphy (North Andover, Mass.: Merrimack College, 1974), 107.

38. Skaggs, "Poe's Shadow," 365–74.

39. James Schroeter, "Willa Cather and *The Professor's House*," *Yale Review* 54 (June 1965): 494–512.

40. Sergeant notes that Cather was quite pleased with *One of Ours*. She recalls: "she had been able to carry out her own intention. In fact she was (critics or not), just discovering how to write; intended (belligerently) to go on learning" (*Memoir*, 172).

41. Jonathan Raban, *The Technique of Modern Fiction: Essays in Practical Criticism* (Notre Dame, Ind.: University of Notre Dame Press, 1969), 35.

42. Cather, "On *Death Comes for the Archbishop*," in *Writing*, 9. In James Woodress's opinion, *"Death Comes for the Archbishop* is the most innovative of all Cather's experiments with the novel form." He adds: "Whether or not it was a novel bothered contemporary reviewers, and Cather herself preferred to call it a narrative" (*Literary Life*, 398–99).

43. Cather, "On *The Professor's House*," in *Writing*, 30–31.

44. Bloom and Bloom, *Gift of Sympathy*, 198.

45. Paul Comeau, "Willa Cather's *Lucy Gayheart*: A Long Perspective," *Prairie Schooner* 55 (Spring-Summer 1981); 208–9.

46. David Stouck, *Willa Cather's Imagination* (Lincoln: University of Nebraska Press, 1975), 1.

47. Skaggs, "Experimental Southern Novel," 3–14.

48. Rosowski, *Voyage Perilous*, 244.

49. Cather, "Art of Fiction," in *Writing*, 102.

50. See James E. Miller, Jr., *F. Scott Fitzgerald: His Art and His Technique* (New York: New York University Press, 1964), for a discussion of Cather's probable influence on Fitzgerald, especially in the manipulation of point of view and the notion of selectivity. In his article "Fitzgerald and Cather: *The Great Gatsby*," *American Literature* 54 (December 1978): 576–91, Tom Quirk reviews the scholarship that demonstrates Cather's influence on Fitzgerald, presents a convincing argument of his own that this influence extends to "matters of incident and story," (576) and also documents Fitzgerald's enthusiasm for, and appreciation of, Cather's style and literary technique.

51. Cather, "Novel Démeublé," in *Forty*, 48–49.

52. Bloom and Bloom, *Gift of Sympathy*, 181.

53. Mona Pers, *Willa Cather's Children* (Stockholm, Sweden: Almquist & Wilhsell International, Uppsala, 1975), 86. Woodress notes that as an adult Cather "clung to the image of childhood as the autonomous, sexless, happy period in life and tried to hang on to her own childhood through dress and memory" (*Literary Life*, 127).

54. Cather, "Prefatory Note," in *Forty*, v.

55. Richard Freedman, *The Novel* (New York: Newsweek Books, 1975), 113.

56. Faulkner, *Modernism*, 14.

57. Josipovici, *Lessons of Modernism*, 109.

58. Cather, "148 Charles Street," in *Forty*, 74.

59. Cather, "On *Death Comes for the Archbishop*" in *Writing*, 12.

60. Cather, "Defoe's *The Fortunate Mistress*," in *Writing*, 84.

61. See in particular T. S. Eliot, "Tradition and the Individual Talent," in *The Sacred Wood: Essays on Poetry and Criticism* (New York: Alfred A. Knopf, 1920). It is interesting that Cather and Eliot shared a publisher, and inconceivable that they were not aware of just what each other was doing in terms of theory.

62. Ellmann and Feidelson, *Modern Traditions*, vi.

63. Stephen Spender, "Moderns and Contemporaries," in *The Idea of the Modern in Literature and the Arts*, ed. Irving Howe (New York: Horizon Press, 1968), 49.

64. Willa Cather, "Nebraska: The End of the First Cycle," *Nation* 117 (5 September 1923): 238.

65. Greene, "Cather at Mid-Century," 589.

66. Eudora Welty, "The House of Willa Cather," in *The Eye of the Story* (New York: Random House, 1977), 43–44. Originally printed in *The Art of Willa Cather*, ed. Bernice Slote and Virginia Faulkner (Lincoln: University of Nebraska Press, 1974), 3–20.

67. Eric Auerbach, *Mimesis* (Princeton: Princeton University Press, 1958), 16.

68. Massey discusses the various ways in which Cather uses juxtaposition in his study of her revisions; he illustrates how she exploits the effect of one word on the other to avoid more elaborate devices. He refers to what he calls her "high-relief technique" as well, which juxtaposes text with space, noting that she was particularly aware of the paragraph break as a form of simplification. The consequent juxtaposition of text and space creates a silence between passages and an emphasis on the opening and closing lines of paragraphs ("Simplicity," 120–21). Woodress records Cather's distress when she was physically unable to write: "Composing by dictation, she wrote, was like playing

solitaire with one's back to the card table. She had to see the words before her eyes; then the thing she was creating took shape on the paper like a picture" (*Literary Life*, 491).

69. Carroll, "Cather," 24.

70. Leo Stein, *Appreciation: Painting, Poetry and Prose* (New York: Crown Publishers, 1947), 74.

71. Linda Pannill, "Willa Cather's Artist-Heroines," *Women's Studies* 11 (December 1984): 230.

72. Cather, "My First Novels," in *Writing*, 97.

73. Faulkner, *Modernism*, 26.

74. Please note that to discuss this point we must rely on metaphor; Cather deals in language—words, not artifacts, and picture-making techniques, not pictures.

Chapter 3. Fiction's Vacuoles

1. Lewis, *Cather Living*, 183.

2. Ibid., 155.

3. Cather, "Novel Démeublé," in *Forty*, 50.

4. Stephen Tennant, "The Room Beyond" in *Writing*, xiv.

5. Lewis, *Cather Living*, 138.

6. Hicks, "Case against Cather," in *Cather and Critics*, 145.

7. Trilling, "Willa Cather," in *After the Genteel Tradition*, ed. Malcolm Cowley (Carbondale: Southern Illinois University Press, 1964), 48.

8. West, "Classic Artist," in *Cather and Critics*, 63.

9. Brown, "Willa Cather," in ibid., 85.

10. Stouck, *Imagination*, 133.

11. Bloom and Bloom, *Gift of Sympathy*, 197–98.

12. Phillip Sheeler and Donald Bianchi, *Cell Biology: Structure, Biochemistry, and Function* (New York: John Wiley & Sons, 1983), 41.

13. Paul J. Kramer, "Problems in Water Relations of Plants and Cells," in *International Review of Cytology*, ed. G. H. Bourne and J. F. Danielli, assist. ed. K. W. Jean (New York: Academic Press, 1983), 263.

14. Joseph G. Hoffman, *The Life and Death of Cells* (Garden City, N.Y.: Hanover House Books, 1957), 27.

15. I. A. Richards, *Principles of Literary Criticism* (New York: Harcourt, Brace & World, 1925), 239.

16. S. M. McGee-Russell, "The Method of Combined Observations with Light and Electron Microscopes Applied to the Study of Histochemical Colourations in Nerve Cells and Oocytes," in *Cell Structure and its Interpretations: Essays Presented to John Randel Baker F. R. S.*, ed. S. M. McGee-Russell and K. F. A. Ross (London: Edward Arnold, 1968), 200.

17. Owen Barfield, *Poetic Diction* (Middletown, Conn.: Wesleyan University Press, 1973), 138.

18. Richards, *Literary Criticism*, 239–40.

19. Sergeant, *Memoir*, 116.

20. Philip Gerber agrees with this assessment: "Had she heard Emily Dickinson say that one knew poetry by the effect it produced—something akin to knowing that the top of one's head had been taken off—she would have been bound to approve, since her own theories rest upon similar recognition" (*Cather*, 13).

21. Barfield, *Poetic Diction*, 48–49.

22. Ibid., 179.

23. Cather, "My First Novels," in *Writing*, 92.

24. Skaggs "Poe's Shadow," 365–74.

25. Willa Cather, *Alexander's Bridge* (Lincoln: University of Nebraska Press, 1977), 112.

26. Slote, "Introduction," in ibid., xxvi.

27. Cather, "My First Novels," in *Writing*, 92–93.

28. Woodress, *Literary Life*, 245.

29. Willa Cather, *O Pioneers!* (Boston: Houghton Mifflin Company, 1941), 75. Subsequent citations from this work are noted parenthetically in the text.

30. Cather, "My First Novels," in *Writing*, 96.

31. Willa Cather, *The Song of the Lark* (Boston: Houghton Mifflin, 1965), iii–iv.

32. Cather, "My First Novels," in *Writing*, 97. Susan Rosowski makes an interesting point: "In many respects it was not until *The Song of the Lark* that Cather came to terms with her heritage. For the first time she used a midwestern point of view and spoke with a midwestern narrative voice. This highly particularized, personal point of view combined with the detailed narrative is the aspect of the novel most criticized; Cather herself believed she had 'taken the wrong road' with her 'full blooded method.' Yet perhaps that fullness was what Cather needed to make her materials her own" (*Voyage Perilous*, 74). We should also recall Cather's own statements regarding the value of her overwritten journalism in developing her later, simpler style.

33. Willa Cather, *My Ántonia* (Boston: Houghton Mifflin Company, 1954), 371. Subsequent citations from this work are noted parenthetically in the text.

34. Willa Cather, interview with Eva Mahoney, "How Willa Cather Found Herself," *Omaha World-Herald*, 27 November 1921, in Bohlke, *Cather in Person*, 39.

35. Woodress, *Literary Life*, 324.

36. This reading of the names in *A Lost Lady* was first presented to me in a seminar discussion by Merrill Maguire Skaggs, Spring 1984.

37. Cather, "On *The Professor's House*," in *Writing*, 31.

38. Louis Kronenberger, "Willa Cather Fumbles for Another Lost Lady," *New York Times Book Review*, 24 October 1926, 2.

39. Willa Cather, *My Mortal Enemy* (New York: Vintage Books, 1954), 48. Subsequent citations from this work are noted parenthetically in the text.

40. Richard Giannone, *Music in Willa Cather's Fiction* (Lincoln: University of Nebraska Presss, 1968), 179–83.

41. Brown and Crone, *Cather*, 130.

42. Randall, *Landscape*, 341.

43. Stouck, *Imagination*, 151.

44. Maxwell Geismar, "Willa Cather: Lady in the Wilderness," in *Cather and Critics*, 194.

45. Having established that Cather uses those intensely remembered scenes from her past to create intensely moving scenes in her writing, we can indicate the source of these drownings. Woodress points out the correspondence between *Alexander's Bridge* and events surrounding the disaster of 1907, which occurred when a bridge under construction near Quebec collapsed, killing eighty men, including the chief engineer, Theodore Cooper (*Literary Life*, 217). We can find ties between the real episode and the fictional account. The emo-

tional intensity with which these drownings are recorded also lies in Cather's own personal experience and her own emotional response to that experience, which she translates into deeply felt art. Willa Cather worked as a columnist in Lincoln with a young man who left for another job in New York. Bernice Slote tells us that "on June 13, 1897, Lincoln learned that Morton Smith had drowned in the Hudson River—his catboat had been hit by a sudden squall and capsized" (*Kingdom of Art*, 25). The effect of this news on Willa Cather is recorded in *Alexander's Bridge* and *Lucy Gayheart*.

46. Lewis, *Cather Living*, 185.

47. Rosowski, *Voyage Perilous*, 239.

Chapter 4. Willa Cather and the "Fine Reader"

1. Bloom and Bloom, *Gift of Sympathy*, 133.

2. Slote, *Kingdom of Art*, 46.

3. Craig, *Foundations*, 171.

4. Cather, "Restlessness," in Bohlke, *Cather in Person*, 68–69.

5. Ezra Pound, "How To Read," *Polite Essays*, (Norfolk, Conn.: New Directions, 1939), 180. Cather believes that one should put less on the page and expect more of the reader's cooperation in divining the unheard overtones of the text.

6. In a letter to Harvey E. Newbranch, published in the *Omaha World-Herald* on 27 October 1929, Cather writes: "I am not lamenting the advent of the 'screen drama' (there is a great deal to be said in its favor), but I do regret that it has put an end to the old-fashioned road companies. . . . The 'movie' and the play are two very different things; one is a play and the other is a picture of a play. A movie, well done, can be very good indeed, may even appeal to what is called the artistic sense; but to the emotions, the deep feelings, never!" (Bohlke, *Cather in Person*, 186). Cather also voiced her main objections to "the modern novel, the cinema, and the radio" in a speech given 14 May 1925 at Bowdoin College: "The novel has resolved into a human convenience to be bought and thrown away at the end of a journey. The cinema has had an almost devastating effect on the theatre. Playwriting goes on about as well as usual, but the cheap and easy substitutes for art are the enemies of art" (155).

7. Cather, "Novel Démeublé," in *Forty*, 43–44.

8. Cather, "Restlessness," in Bohlke, *Cather in Person*, 69.

9. Cather, "Jewett," in *Forty*, 92.

10. Ibid., 94.

11. Anne Smith, "Introduction," in Ackroyd, *New Culture*, 7.

12. Ellmann and Feidelson, *Modern Tradition*, vi.

13. Frank Lentricchia, *After the New Criticism* (Chicago: University of Chicago Press, 1980), 185.

14. Throckmorton, "Cather," 215, 217.

15. Cather, "Art of Fiction," in *Writing*, 102.

16. George William Greene, "Willa Cather's Grand Manan," *Prairie Schooner* (Spring-Summer 1981): 240

17. Arthur Koestler, "Character and Identification" in *Insight and Outlook* (New York: The Macmillan Company, 1949), 363.

18. George Szanto, *Narrative Consciousness* (Austin: University of Texas, 1972), 4.

19. Robert Crosman, "Do Readers Make Meaning?," in *The Reader in the*

Text, eds. Susan Suleiman and Inge Crosman (Princeton: Princeton University Press, 1980), 164.

20. Cather, "Jewett," in *Forty*, 78.

21. Cather, "Light on Adobe Walls," in *Writing*, 124.

22. Leon Edel, *Willa Cather, The Paradox of Success*, a lecture delivered in 1959. (Washington Reference Dept., Library of Congress, 1960), 6.

23. Among the works that present the spectrum of criticism regarding the reader's role in the interpretation of literature are: Robert Graves and Alan Hodge, *The Reader Over Your Shoulder* (New York: Collier Books, 1966); Roger Fowler, ed., *Style and Structure in Literature: Essays in the New Stylistics* (Ithaca: N.Y.: Cornell University Press, 1975); Susan Suleiman and Inge Crosman, eds. *The Reader in the Text* (Princeton: Princeton University Press, 1980); Jane Tompkins, ed., *Reader-Response Criticism: From Formalism to Post-Structuralism*, (Baltimore: Johns Hopkins University Press, 1980); Steven Mailliux, *Interpretive Conventions: The Reader in the Study of Americn Fiction* (Ithaca: Cornell University Press, 1982). Four full-length discussions of the reader's construction of literature have proved to be of great help in understanding Willa Cather's relationship with her reader. They are Roman Ingarden, *The Cognition of the Literary Work of Art*, trans. Ruth Ann Crowley and Kenneth R. Olsen (Evanston: Northwestern University Press, 1973); Wolfgang Iser, *The Act of Reading* (London: Routledge & Kegan Paul, 1979) and *The Implied Reader* (Baltimore: Johns Hopkins University Press, 1974); and Horst Ruternof, *The Reader's Construction of Narrative* (London: Routledge & Kegan Paul, 1981).

24. James Woodress, *Willa Cather: Her Life and Art* (New York: Pegasus, 1970), 201.

25. Robert Scholes and Robert Kellogg, "The Problem of Reality: Illustration and Representation," in *Theory of Novel*, 371.

26. These techniques might also apply to Joseph Conrad (whom Cather admired) in his novels and to Ford Madox Ford (whom Cather knew and hated, calling him the prince of prevaricators) in his descriptions of "impressionism" in fiction. Conrad and Ford were both influenced by Flaubert and James, and their emphasis on making the reader "see" has its parallel in Cather's development.

27. Cather, "Joseph and His Brothers," in *Forty*, 102.

28. Raban, *Techniques*, 101. It has been well documented by Cather's biographers that Cather had read widely in the classics—Homer, Virgil, even the Norse myths; that she had a working knowledge of the Bible and the great allegorical works such as *Pilgrim's Progress;* that she was a voracious reader of both "popular" and "quality" writing; and that she loved and knew the great operas and the traditions from which they came. It is not surprising, therefore, to find in the work reference to the systems that we recognize, and also to codes and systems that are more esoteric, such as the Victorian language of flowers and the significance of certain gems.

29. Merrill Maguire Skaggs illustrates Cather's use of this technique in *Sapphira and the Slave Girl* in her article "Willa Cather's Experimental Southern Novel." Skaggs indicates both the expected, traditional plot and character conventions according to many commonly held beliefs about Southern codes and the way in which Cather twists each around; readers must reconsider the convention they expected, the situation they get, and their reaction to the difference between the two. Another study of the reversal of reader expectation is Frederick Griffiths, "The Woman Warrior: Willa Cather and *One of Ours*,"

Women's Studies 11 (December 1984); 261–85, in which he points out "an Eve who seduces by frigidity, an Adam who lapses through obedience, soldiers who fantasize less about killing than about giving birth, and at the center a controlling image of the woman warrior, most obviously, Jeanne d'Arc" (263). Susan Rosowski's "*O Pioneers!* Willa Cather's New World Pastoral" provides an illuminating discussion of Cather's use of pastoral and myth, in which she demonstrates that "like the moderns, Cather places her characters within myths that are inadequate or that disintegrate, leaving them helpless. Emil and Marie in the orchard recall Adam and Eve in the Garden, but with enormous differences: by making the orchard lapsed and Marie a married woman, Cather makes a 'fit' between characters and myth impossible" *Voyage Perilous*, (56).

30. J. Bronowski, *Science and Human Values*, (New York: Harper and Son, 1956), 27.

31. Cather, "Joseph and His Brothers," in *Forty*, 119. Cather also used other storyteller's stories that were present in her reader's consciousness, however. As Marilyn Berg Callander demonstrates in *Willa Cather and the Fairy Tale* (Ann Arbor: UMI Research Press, 1988), Cather used fairy tales extensively as reference points for her readers. We would also suggest that she uses them to evoke that common fund of knowledge that allows readers to participate in the creative act.

32. Zabel, *Craft and Character*, 275.

33. Norman Friedman, "Point of View in Fiction: The Development of a Critical Concept" in *Theory of Novel*, 132–33.

34. Letter to Mr. Miller, 24 October 1924, Willa Cather/Benjamin Hitz collection, The Newberry Library, Chicago.

35. Stouck, *Imagination*, 59.

36. Sharon O'Brien, "Mothers, Daughters and the 'Art Necessity': Willa Cather and the Creative Process," in *American Novelists Revisited: Essays in Feminist Criticism* ed. Fritz Fleishman (Boston: Hall, 1982), 286.

37. Ellen Moers, *Literary Women: The Great Writers* (Garden City, N.Y.: Doubleday, 1976), 238.

38. Leonard Lutwack, "Mixed and Uniform Prose Styles in the Novel," in *Theory of Novel*, 218.

39. Susan J. Rosowski, "Willa Cather—A Pioneer in Art: *O Pioneers!* and *My Ántonia*," *Prairie Schooner* 55 (Spring-Summer 1981): 142.

40. René Rapin, *Willa Cather* (New York: R. M. McBride, 1930), 85.

41. Welty, "House of Cather," in *Eye of Story*, 41–42.

42. Benjamin B. Hampton, "The Author and the Motion Picture," *Bookman* 53 (May 1921): 221.

43. Woodress, *Literary Life*, 352. We also learn from Woodress that during the Depression when her Nebraska friends were in desperate straits, she was willing to sell *The Song of the Lark*, if she could get a good enough price (437). Considering her later concern that "the Goddam movies were after *My Ántonia*; she was living in terror that Houghton Mifflin would sell her out" (478), we can see what a sacrifice she was willing to make for those she loved, remembered, and supported in bad times.

44. Letter to Harvey E. Newbranch, in Bohlke, *Cather in Person*, 186.

45. Charles Eidsvik, *Cineliteracy: Film among the Arts* (New York: Random House, 1978), 284.

46. In his article, "Hemingway as *Auteur*," *The South Atlantic Quarterly* 86 (Spring 1987): 151–58, Peter L. Hays also discusses "what is cinematic about

Hemingway's writing," (156) and, in doing so, touches on many of the characteristics we also find in Cather's prose: the objectivity of presentation, the use of sensory detail to trigger an emotional response, and the demands that such a style makes on the reader. I would suggest that Hemingway was influenced by Cather's experimentation with these very techniques, just as Fitzgerald was influenced by her work, but, rather than acknowledge such a debt, instead chose to denigrate Cather's work.

47. Alan Speigel, *Fiction and the Camera Eye* (Charlottesville: University of Virginia Press, 1976), xi.

48. Louis Giannetti, *Understanding Movies* (Englewood Cliffs, N.J.: Prentice-Hall, 1982), 194.

49. Ibid., 324.

50. Eidsvik, *Cineliteracy*, 230.

51. David A. Cook, *A History of Narrative Film* (New York: W. W. Norton, 1981), 625.

52. Speigel, *Fiction*, 6.

53. Ibid., 7.

54. Ibid., 19.

55. Ibid., 7. Harold Toliver discusses Hemingway's "cinematic" technique in his book, *Animate Illusions: Explorations of Narrative Structure* (Lincoln: University of Nebraska Press, 1974), saying that he uses juxtaposition, repetition, minimal dialogue, and minimal description. He does not mention Cather.

56. Ibid., 26.

57. Cather, "Novel Démeublé," in *Forty*, 45. "The art of choosing among the innumerable strokes which nature offers us is, after all, much more difficult than that of observing them with attention and rendering them with exactitude" (my translation).

58. Cather, "Stephen Crane's *Wounds in the Rain* and Other Impressions of War," in *Writing*, 69–70.

59. Skaggs, "Experimental Southern Novel," 11.

60. Cather, "Defoe's *The Fortunate Mistress*," in *Writing*, 79.

61. Comeau, *"Lucy Gayheart,"* 199.

62. Daiches, *Cather*, 132.

63. Hemingway's remarks were contained in a letter to Edmund Wilson on 25 November 1923, which Wilson quotes in *The Shores of Light: A Literary Chronicle of the Twenties and Thirties* (New York: Farrar, Straus, and Young, 1952): "Look at *One of Ours*. . . . Prize, big sale, people taking it seriously. You were in the war weren't you? Wasn't that last scene in the lines wonderful? Do you know where it came from? The battle scene in *Birth of a Nation*. I identified episode after episode, Catherized. Poor woman, she had to get her war experience somewhere" (118).

64. Griffiths, "Woman Warrior," 264. Interestingly, Peter Hays documents that Hemingway was the one familiar with *Birth of a Nation*; James Woodress has pointed out to me that the only movies Cather's letters even report her seeing and liking are those starring Rin-Tin-Tin.

65. Rapin, *Cather*, 56.

66. Cather, "Restlessness" in Bohlke, *Cather in Person*, 69.

67. The characteristic juxtaposition of word, details, scenes, and episodes that account for so much of the compression and submerged meaning within the novels also appears as an organizational force in her short story collections. Philip Gerber explains: "One expects the principle of juxtaposition to operate

in Cather's story collections, where separate tales serve to develop aspects of the major theme that binds them all together. She produced only three collections in her lifetime, and her selectivity in determining what would be saved assured their unity. Each story becomes a 'panel' in a larger work, but that the same principle operates in her novels is less often recognized" (*Cather*, 146).

68. Ingarden, *Literary Work*, 354.

69. Iser, *Reading*, 225.

70. Ruternof, *Construction of Narrative*, 187.

71. Iser, *Reading*, 186.

72. Karlheinz Stierle, "The Reading of Fictional Texts," in *Reader in Text*, 105.

73. We should note here the recently translated theories of Russian thinker Mikhail Bakhtin, *The Dialogic Imagination*, ed. Michael Holquist, trans. Caryl Emerson and Michael Holquist (Austin: University of Texas Press, 1981), dealing with language, the study of the novel, and the relationship of the reader to the text. Distinguishing between the real and the represented worlds, between the "listener or reader of multiple and varied periods, recreating and renewing the text" and "the passive listener or reader of one's own time" (253), Bakhtin states: "The work and the world represented in it enter the real world and enrich it, and the real world enters the work and its world as part of the process of its creation, as well as part of its subsequent life, in a continual renewing of the work through the creative perception of listeners and readers" (254). Joseph C. Murphy has used Bakhtin's distinction between "monologic" discourse (which privileges one absolute version of reality over all others) and "dialogic" discourse (which presents a dialogue among differing perceptions with no one perception valorized) in his article "*Shadows on the Rock* and *To the Lighthouse*—A Bakhtinian Perspective," *Willa Cather Pioneer Memorial Newsletter* 31 (Summer 1987): 31–36.

Chapter 5. *A Lost Lady*

1. Massey, "Simplicity," 10.

2. Cather, "Jewett," in *Forty*, 78–79.

3 Joseph Wood Krutch, "Reviews of Four Novels—The Lady as Artist," in Schroeter, *Cather and Critics*, 53.

4. Hicks, "Case against Cather," in ibid., 143.

5. Rapin, *Cather*, 71.

6. Rosowski, *Voyage Perilous*, 116.

7. Cather, "Escapism," in *Writing*, 27.

8. In "Nebraska: The End of the First Cycle," Cather wrote: "When I stop at one of the graveyards in my own county and see on the headstones the names of the fine old men I used to know: 'Eric Ericson, born Bergen, Norway . . . died Nebraska,' 'Anton Pucelik, born Prague, Bohemia . . . died Nebraska,' I have always the hope that something went into the ground with those pioneers that will one day come out again. Something that will come out not only in sturdy traits of character, but in elasticity of mind, in an honest attitude toward the realities of life, in certain qualities of feeling and imagination" (237).

9. Martin Foss, *Symbol and Metaphor in Human Experience* (Princeton: Princeton University Press, 1942), 62.

10. Cather, "Jewett," in *Forty*, 91.

11. George Snell makes this same point in his book, *The Shapers of American Fiction* (New York: Cooper Square Publishers, 1961): "In many respects it [*A Lost Lady*] is one of the best-realized short novels in our literature, and it is certainly more truly 'American' than any of the equally fine novelettes by Henry James, with which it can often stand comparison" (154).

12. Gerber, *Cather*, 111. This interview with Flora Merrill, "A Short Story Course Can Only Delay," *New York World*, 19 April 1925, sec. 6, 6, is reprinted in Bohlke, *Cather in Person*, 73–80.

13. Edmund Wilson, "Two Novels of Willa Cather," in *Cather and Critics*, 28.

14. Friedman, "Point of View," in *Theory of Novel*, 113–14.

15. Willa Cather, *A Lost Lady* (New York: Vintage Books,1972), 86. Subsequent citations from this work are noted parenthetically in the text. This scene also presents an excellent example of the function of the vacuole in the juxtaposition of two images: Niel bending to lay the flowers at the window, and Niel standing breathless on the wooden bridge. The gap between the sentences "And it was fat and lazy—ended in something like a yawn" and "Niel found himself at the foot of the hill on the wooden bridge" emphasized by a paragraph break between them as well reproduces for the reader that instant of horrible realization, as the first image impinges on the second.

16. Szanto, *Narrative Consciousness*, 156.

17. Wayne C. Booth, "Distance and Point of View," in *Theory of Novel*, 98–99.

18. Stouck points to Cather's decision to rewrite the book in third-person narration as "crucial, for the use of the third person allows the introduction of an ironic perspective into the story simultaneously with the romantic view of its protagonist" (*Imagination*, 59). I would suggest that Cather was equally interested in keeping the reader's attention focused on Marian and in keeping the reader's imagination involved in an interactive reading of the text.

19. Sharon O'Brien attributes Cather's control of "consistent and unerring" authorial distance to her choice of third-person narration in "Mothers, Daughters, and the 'Art Necessity': Willa Cather and the Creative Process" in *American Novelists Revisited: Essays in Feminist Criticism* ed. by Fritz Fleishman (Boston: Hall, 1982), 287.

20. Josipovici, "Linearity and Fragmentation," in *Lessons of Modernism*, 124. In "Hip-Deep in Post-modernism," Todd Gitlin also points out the correlation between the use of fragmentation and what we now call modernism: "In modernism, voices, perspectives and material were multiple. The unity of the work was assembled from fragments and juxtapositions. Art set out to remake life. Audacious individual style threw off the dead hand of the past. Continuity was disrupted, the individual subject dislocated" (*The New York Times Book Review*, 6 November 1988, 35).

21. Randall, *Landscape*, 175.

22. Faulkner, *Modernism*, 14.

23. Cather, "Nebraska: End of First Cycle," 236.

24. Iser, *Reading*, 121.

25. Hatcher, *Creating American Novel*, 10.

26. Nancy Morrow, "Willa Cather's *A Lost Lady* and the Nineteenth-Century Novel of Adultery," *Women's Studies* 11 (December 1984): 294.

27. A case can be made for understanding the novel in terms of Marian as Niel's surrogate mother. Niel vacillates between a child's view of Marian and

a lover's. Because Niel's own mother had died—and Niel refers to her as "Poor lady" (30)—he may very well choose Marian as a mother substitute. This ambiguity suggests an incestuous relationship. Perhaps we should see Marian as Jocasta; Niel says that "No other house could take the place of this one in his life" (142). A different, yet most intriguing, reading is offered by Ellen Moers: "Prairie pastoral! *A Lost Lady* is an Electra story, raw and barbarous. Marian Forrester is a queen and a whore as well. She has betrayed the king—that traveler and conqueror of the West, the old impotent railroad man Captain Forrester. Her various seductions and adulteries both inflame and revolt young Niel, who is as impotent in revenge as he is in lust" (238).

28. Morrow, *"Lost Lady* and Adultery," 296–97.

29. Iser, *Reading*, 208.

30. Lionel Trilling records Sinclair Lewis's Nobel Prize Speech to illustrate this seeming lapse in moral education: "So would you have been told that Miss Willa Cather, for all the homely virtue of her novels concerning the peasants of Nebraska, has in her novel, *A Lost Lady*, been so untrue to America's patent and perpetual and posssibly tedious virtuousness as to picture an abandoned woman who remains, nevertheless, uncannily charming even to the virtuous, in a story without any moral" ("Willa Cather," in *After the Genteel Tradition*, 7–8). Thomas Uzzell considers *A Lost Lady* a faulty novel because, as he insists, "a writer should not attempt a theme unless he intends to grapple with it. A novel about evil must picture the evil" (*Technique*, 238). What Lewis does not point out and what Uzzell does not understand is that in the book virtue itself is relative to the consciousness defining it. These perceptions are not measured against any rigid authorial standard; therefore the reader's standard of virtue colors his or her version of the story.

31. Stouck, *Imagination*, 72.

32. Cather readily admits to "borrowing" in her essay "Gertrude Hall's *The Wagnerian Romances.*" She says: "If you wish to know how difficult it is to transfer the feeling of an operatic scene upon a page of narrative, try it! I had to attempt it once, in the course of a novel, and I paid Miss Hall the highest compliment one writer can pay another; I stole from her" (*Writing*, 64–65).

33. Cather, "Chance Meeting," in *Forty*, 20.

34. We must note that Cather scholars have done considerable work pointing out other parallels in her work. See Skaggs, "Poe's Shadow," and John J. Murphy, "Euripides' *Hippolytus* and Cather's *A Lost Lady*," *American Literature* 53 (March 1981): 72–86, for example.

35. Gustave Flaubert, quoted in Ackroyd, *New Culture*, 19.

36. Bloom and Bloom, *Gift of Sympathy*, 184.

37. Raban, *Technique*, 169.

38. Matthew J. Bruccoli, "'An Instance of Apparent Plagiarism': F. Scott Fitzgerald, Willa Cather, and the First *Gatsby* Manuscript," *Princeton University Library Chronicle* 39 (1978): 171–72, 176. Tom Quirk tells us that when he received Cather's letter, "Fitzgerald was understandably excited about the letter, so much so that he woke up Christian Gausse and his wife at one 'o'clock in the morning to celebrate" (576).

39. The opal's association with bad luck arises from its identification as the stone of the Goddess in the old, repressed, and denounced goddess religions that the Church has considered immoral and heretical because of their nature centeredness. Thirteen is also unlucky because it is the goddess's number—the number of actual lunar months (or moons) in the calendar year. We might, then,

suggest that this reference to opals—and the references to the new moon as well—refer to a more "basic," natural, amoral (by Christian standards) and goddess-centered point of view.

40. Other specific references are also useful to understand how Cather used every available bit of suggestive detail. When Niel goes to the Forresters' house after the blizzard, the Captain shows him hyacinths and narcissus. The heavy odor of narcissus, worn by the Furies, is reputed to cause headaches and even madness, and the hyacinth, as legend has it, sprang from the blood of the beautiful youth Hyacinthus, slain by Apollo (Alice M. Coats, *Flowers and Their Histories* [New York: McGraw-Hill, 1968]).

41. Woodress, *Literary Life*, 343.

Chapter 6. *The Professor's House*

1. Lionel Trilling, in *Genteel Tradition*, 57.

2. Krutch, "Reviews of Four Novels," in *Cather and Critics*, 56.

3. Alfred Kazin, *On Native Grounds* (New York: Reynal & Hitchcock, 1942), 255. Although more recent criticism has dealt less harshly with the novel's experimental structure, the novel, nevertheless, has had little appeal for a wide audience. As late as 1965, James Schroeter wrote: "This book is not so well known as some of her others. It has not appeared in paper, and has escaped the college vogue that has kept other books of the same era—*The Great Gatsby*, *The Sun Also Rises*—in the public eye. But it is an interesting, vigorous, thought-provoking book, perhaps Willa Cather's most interesting, and one of the significant American novels of the twentieth century" ("Cather and *Professor's House*," 499).

4. Merrill Maguire Skaggs, "A Glance into *The Professor's House*: Inward and Outward Bound," *Renascence* 39 (Spring 1987): 422.

5. Elizabeth Moorhead, "The Novelist," in *Cather and Critics*, 112.

6. Cather, "On *The Professor's House*" in *Writing*, 31.

7. In his article "The Literary Endeavor of Willa Cather (As Inspired by Joan Crane's Bibliography)," *Willa Cather Pioneer Memorial Newsletter* 32 (Fall 1988): 33–37, Jack Collins reminds us of just how avant-garde this book was: "she conceived the subjects and structures of her novels in pictorial terms. . . . What is most original about all this is that her visual way of thinking enables her to perceive fictional structures spatially. The planes in her pictures, as it were, can be blocks of narrative. Woolf's *To The Lighthouse* (1927) makes virtuoso use of such a conception of narrative. Yet the central panel of narrative "Tom Outland's Story" in *The Professor's House*, a work virtually obscure in comparison to Woolf's novel, achieves the same effect as the famous "Time Passes" two years before Woolf presents her own experiment to the public" (36).

8. Cather "On *The Professor's House*," in *Writing* 31–32. This excerpt is from a letter written in 1938, thirteen years after the book was published. We should notice that Cather's memory of her experience of the painting, seen before she wrote *The Professor's House*, is intensely real to her and effectively conveyed in her correspondence.

9. This example is not the only one in which Cather uses this technique. In *My Ántonia, Death Comes for the Archbishop*, and *Sapphira and the Slave Girl*, she uses inset narrative to emphasize the major plot and thematic develop-

ments. In this novel, she uses the most radical form—breaking the narrative structure completely—to make her point.

10. Ackroyd, *New Culture*, 147.

11. Bloom and Bloom, "Poetics of Cather," in *Five Essays*, 107.

12. We must not go any further without noting that the sea, window and crowded room are all the products of art. They are real as art, and as art they elicit a response. Cather remarks on the feeling of the sea that she got from the juxtaposition of the sea with the room; we must remember that she considered the true measure of art to be its ability to arouse emotion. See Chapter 4.

13. Daiches, *Cather*, 88.

14. Yongue "Cather's Creative Process," 13.

15. Henry Steele Commager says: "Better than any of her literary contemporaries, she represented the force of tradition in twentieth-century America—the tradition of the artist, the tradition of the pioneer, the tradition, eventually, of the universal church" (*The American Mind* [New Haven: Yale University Press, 1950], 155). He does not, however, consider the high-relief technique of juxtaposing these traditions with contemporary American values, which is so much a part of Cather's art.

16. Like many of the European-identified American modernists, Cather seems to reject the immediate past and to identify with a lost or forgotten culture that must be recovered. She chose a different ancient culture than Joyce or Pound and, in doing so, offers the hope that the values of *her* lost culture may, in fact, be found in the few steady souls who have maintained the tradition.

17. Gerber, *Cather*, 156–57.

18. Wagenknecht, *American Novel*, 337.

19. Welty, "House of Cather," *Eye of Story*, 47.

20. Willa Cather, *The Professor's House* (New York: Vintage, 1973), 253. Subsequent citations from this work are noted parenthetically in the text.

21. Welty, "House of Cather," in *Eye of Story*, 57.

22. Iser, *Reading*, 188.

23. Ibid., 203.

24. Stierle, "Fictional Texts," in *Reader in Text*, 100–1.

25. Cather, "Restlessness," in Bohlke, *Cather in Person*, 69.

26. Cather, "Defoe's *Fortunate Mistress*," in *Writing*, 79–80. See chapter 4.

27. Cather, "Defoe's *Fortunate Mistress*," in *Writing*, 78.

28. Willa Cather, interview with Ethel Hockett, "The Vision of a Successful Fiction Writer," *Lincoln Daily Star*, 24 October 1915, in Bohlke, *Cather in Person*, 15.

29. Uzzell, *Techniques*, 20.

30. Mérimée, quoted in Cather "Novel Démeublé," in *Forty*, 45. The quotation appears in French: "L'art de chosir parmi les innombrables traits que nous offre la nature est, après tout, bien plus difficile que celui de les observer avec attention et de les rendre avec exactitude."

31. Letter to Irene Miner Weisz, 17 February 1925, Willa Cather–Irene Weisz correspondence, The Newberry Library, Chicago.

32. Sergeant, *Memoir*, 156–57.

33. To make the statement that Willa Cather was directly influenced by Marcel Proust seems unjust to both writers. I would rather suggest that Cather experimented with techniques that she noticed in Proust's work to serve her own purposes. I also believe, however, that she shared a certain modern attitude

toward the uses of detail, scene, and juxtaposition of time frames with her French contemporary. As we saw earlier, she is not above admitting to "borrowing" from other writers. Here she does give us an oblique comment that I believe refers to Proust, though it is entirely appropriate to the design and intent of the story as well. When Roddy sells the artifacts to the German, Tom compares him to Dreyfus. Roddy responds: "That man was innocent. It was a frame-up" (243). Marcel Proust worked diligently for the release of Dreyfus, risking social ostracism by circulating petitions and assisting Dreyfus's lawyer.

34. Kronenberger, "Cather," 135.

35. Sergeant, *Memoirs*, 107.

36. Sarah Orne Jewett, quoted by Cather in "Jewett," in *Forty*, 76.

37. The Professor's recognition of his childhood self also reminds us of Cather's notion that a child has the ability to perceive nuances unavailable to the adult. Here, she refers to the "vivid consciousness of an earlier state" (264) that comes back to the Professor, and she makes the provocative statement that "adolescence grafted a new creature into the original one, and that the complexion of a man's life was largely determined by how well or ill his original self and his nature as modified by sex rubbed on together" (266–67).

38. W. T. Noon, "Modern Literature and the Sense of Time," *Thought* 33 (September 1973); 581.

39. Giannetti, *Movies*, 136.

40. Ackroyd, *New Culture*, 105.

41. Edwin Muir, *The Structure of the Novel* (London: The Hogarth Press, 1954), 103.

42. Foss, *Symbol and Metaphor*, 115.

43. Bronowski, *Science*, 19.

Chapter 7. *My Mortal Enemy*

1. Cather, "Novel Démeublé," in *Forty*, p. 51.

2. Ibid., 51.

3. Brown, *Cather* 250.

4. Slote, *Kingdom of Art*, 46.

5. Woodress, *Literary Life*, 380.

6. Randall, *Landscape*, 239.

7. Lina Mainiero, ed., *American Women Writers* (New York: Frederick Unger, 1979), 318.

8. Stouck, *Imagination*, 120.

9. Fanny Butcher tells us that Cather was pleased with her review of *My Mortal Enemy* because "it was worth writing a book to have someone get the point of it absolutely, and what she had written about was, as I had said, that fundamental, both the attraction and antagonism between two strongly individual people who love deeply, truly, the irresistible attraction of being one, and the final resentment at no longer being two unentangled individuals" (*Many Lives*, 361). Woodress paraphrases a letter Cather wrote in 1940: "She was always glad, she wrote, when people told her they liked the nouvelle because it had been rather difficult to write. Her correspondent had wanted to know why two very minor characters, Ewan Grey and Esther Sinclair, did not reenter the story. They had appeared in the Madison Square chapters to illustrate one aspect of Myra's character—her propensity to help young lovers overcome ob-

stacles even though, as she put it 'very likely hell will come of it!' Cather explained patiently that she was painting a portrait of Myra with reflections of her in various looking glasses. It would have been foolish to try to account for any of the people Myra had loved and left behind. It was the extravagance of her devotions that made her in the end feel that Oswald was her mortal enemy, that he had somehow been the enemy of her soul's peace. Her soul, of course, could never have been at peace. She wasn't that kind of woman" (*Literary Life*, 384–85). Cather's old friend, George Seibel, recalls that when he asked if Oswald was Myra's enemy, she answered, "Of course, you are quite right. I can't see much in this particular story unless you get the point of it. There is not much to it but the point!" ("Miss Willa Cather From Nebraska," *New Colophon* 2 [September 1949]: 207). Cather does not, however, add that there can be many points to every one of her books.

10. Moers, *Literary Women*, 233.

11. Merrill Maguire Skaggs, "*My Mortal Enemy*: Willa Cather's *Tour de Force*," MS.

12. Gerber, *Cather*, 117.

13. Rosowski, *Voyage Perilous*, 154.

14. E. K. Brown tells us: "Although the story was awkwardly short for a book, Willa Cather believed that it should appear by itself, that it was in fact a book. She had misgivings about the judgment Alfred A. Knopf would pass. Twenty years later she still spoke with enthusiasm of his quick response to *My Mortal Enemy*. He made no difficulty about publishing it as it was, and his opinion was speedily ratified by the sales, which required five printings before the end of 1926, and by the closeness with which the critics discussed a psychological portrait that was felt to be sharp and original, if at points a little mystifying" (*Cather*, 248).

15. Cather, "Jewett," in *Forty*, 78.

16. Josephine L. Jessup, *The Faith of Our Feminists* (New York: Richard R. Smith, 1950), 66.

17. Giannone, *Music in Cather's Fiction*, 181.

18. Ibid., 178.

19. Stouck, *Imagination*, 127.

20. Harry B. Eichorn, "A Falling Out with Love: *My Mortal Enemy*," *Colby Library Quarterly* 10 (September 1973): 132.

21. These ideas were first suggested to me in Merrill Skaggs's Willa Cather seminar, Spring 1984. Though Rosowski does not use the term *suicide*, she points out that "Myra dies at a carefully conducted ceremony in which she officiates over her own rites" (*Voyage Perilous*, 152). We should also mention that this reading of Myra's death as suicide has been anticipated three times: Myra has Nellie read her the poem "about the flower that grows on the suicide's grave, *die Armesunderblum*', the poor-sinner's-flower" (80); Myra's surrogate son, Billy, shoots himself over a "sordid love affair" (86); and Myra exclaims, "Oh, let me be buried in the king's highway!" (92). Every detail has been carefully selected to add greater meaning to the story.

22. Ann Moseley, "The Voyage Perilous: Willa Cather's Mythic Quest," Ph.D. diss., University of Oklahoma, 1974, 254. We should also point out that violet—Myra's color—and yellow—Oswald's color—are complementary, producing pure white when combined. See also Kathryn T. Stofer, "Gems and Jewelry: Cather's Imagery in *My Mortal Enemy*," *Willa Cather Pioneer Memorial Newsletter* 30 (Summer 1986): 19–22.

23. Wilber M. Urban, *Language and Reality: The Philosophy of Language and the Principles of Symbolism* (London: B. Allen & Unwin, 1939), 463.

24. Susan J. Rosowski, "Narrative Technique in Cather's *My Mortal Enemy*," *Journal of Narrative Technique* 8 (Spring 1978): 141–44.

25. Booth, "Point of View," in *Theory of Novel*, 98–99.

26. Nellie uses five name variations for both Myra and Oswald in the novel. She uses Myra twenty-nine times, Mrs. Henshawe twenty-eight times, Myra Henshawe eight times, Mrs. Myra seven times, and Myra Driscoll three times. In addition, she calls Oswald by his given name twenty-six times, Henshawe eight times, Oswald Henshawe four times, Young Oswald two times, and Mr. Henshawe two times.

27. Schroeter, *Cather and Critics*, 23.

28. Iser, *Reading*, 196.

29. My emphasis throughout this discussion of voice change.

Conclusion

1. Cather, "Light on Adobe Walls," in *Writing*, 125.

2. Howard N. Doughty, Jr., "Miss Cather as Critic," *Nation* 169 (24 September 1947): 304.

3. Cather, "Jewett," in *Forty*, 76–77.

4. Daiches, *Cather*, 14.

5. Cather, "Jewett," in *Forty*, 77–78.

6. Foss, *Symbol and Metaphor*, 122.

7. Sergeant, *Memoir*, 19.

8. Randall, *Landscape* xi.

9. Massey, "Simplicity," 107.

10. Sergeant, *Memoir*, 203.

11. Pound "How to Read," in *Polite Essays*, 23.

12. Sergeant, *Memoir*, 133.

13. Cather, "Christina Rossetti," *Nebraska State Journal*, 13 January 1895, in Slote, *Kingdom of Art*, 348.

14. Welty, "House of Cather," in *Eye of Story*, 53.

15. Willa Cather, interview with Eleanor Hinman, *Lincoln Sunday Star*, 6 November 1921, in Bohlke, *Cather in Person*, 47.

16. Richard Giannone, *Music in Willa Cather's Fiction* (Lincoln: University of Nebraska Press, 1968); Joseph X. Brennen, "Willa Cather and Her Music," *University Review* 31 (Spring 1965): 175–83, and "Music and Willa Cather," *University Review* 32 (Summer 1965): 257–64.

17. Welty, "House of Cather," in *Eye of Story*, 41.

18. Bloom and Bloom, "Poetics of Cather," in *Five Essays*, 109.

19. Willa Cather, Inscription on a photograph dated 16 February 1920, quoted in Butcher, *Many Lives*, 356.

20. Cather, "Restlessness," in Bohlke, *Cather in Person*, 72.

21. Daiches, *Cather*, 29.

22. Throckmorton, "Cather," 62. Cather revised *The Song of the Lark* for republication in 1932, cutting out about seven thousand words. James Woodress suggests that "she must have decided on looking over the book more than two decades after writing it that major surgery was inadvisable and it was best to let the novel stand pretty much as it was" (273). For a detailed discussion see

Robin Heyeck and James Woodress, "Willa Cather's Cuts and Revisions in *The Song of the Lark*," *Modern Fiction Studies* (Winter 1979–80): 651–58.

23. We must note that Cather's rendition of the Ancient People in *The Song of the Lark* anticipates the Cliff Dwellers of *The Professor's House*. The differences between the two accounts illustrate the differences between the démeublé style and Cather's experimental full-blooded method.

24. Woodress, *Life and Art*, 180.

25. James E. Miller, *Quests Surd and Absurd* (Chicago: University of Chicago Press, 1967), 67.

26. Cather, "How Cather Found Herself" in Bohlke, *Cather in Person*, 39.

27. In discussing Cather's ability to involve the reader on any one of several levels, depending on his or her sensitivity to suggestion, Griffiths cites the scene in which the German soldier is killed: "This passage epitomizes Cather's tact in addressing several audiences at once. Those like Sergeant who prefer to see no sex, need see none. The curious can deduce from Claude's obtuseness about homosexuality that his relationship with David, though shaped in many ways by sexual feelings, has never been physical, . . . Cather's tableau juxtaposes the oldest homoerotic stereotype in Western literature—the soldier lovers (cf. Gilgamesh and Enkidu, Achilles and Patroclus)—to the newest: the pervert" ("Woman Warrior," 267).

28. Butcher, *Many Lives*, 359.

29. Jessup, *Faith of Feminists*, 69.

30. Woodress, *A Literary Life*, 406.

31. Slote, *Kingdom of Art*. 43.

32. Lentricchia, *New Criticism*, 58.

Bibliography

Books

Ackroyd, Peter. *Notes for a New Culture: An Essay on Modernism*. New York: Barnes & Noble, 1976.

Allen, Walter. *The Urgent West*. New York: E. P. Dutton, 1969.

Arnold, M. *Willa Cather's Short Fiction*. Athens: Ohio University Press, 1984.

Auchincloss, Louis. *Pioneers and Caretakers: A Study of Nine American Women Writers*. Minneapolis: University of Minnesota Press, 1965.

Auerbach, Eric. *Mimesis*. Princeton: Princeton University Press, 1958.

Austin, John L. *How To Do Things with Words*. London: Oxford University Press, 1962.

Bakhtin, M. M. *The Dialogic Imagination*. Edited by Michael Holquist. Translated by Caryl Emerson and Michael Holquist. Austin: University of Texas Press, 1981.

Balakian, Anna E. *The Symbolist Movement*. New York: Random House, 1967.

Barfield, Owen. *Poetic Diction*. Middletown, Conn.: Wesleyan University Press, 1973.

Baym, Max I. *A History of Literary Aesthetics in America*. New York: Frederick Unger, 1973.

Bennett, Mildred R. *My Ántonia: Notes*. Lincoln, Neb.: Cliffs Notes, 1962.

——*The World of Willa Cather*. Lincoln: University of Nebraska Press, 1961.

Bett, Henry. *Some Secrets of Style*. London: G. Allen and Unwin, 1932.

Bloom, Edward A., and Lillian D. *Willa Cather's Gift of Sympathy*. Carbondale: Southern Illinois University Press, 1962.

Bluestone, George. *Novels into Film*. Baltimore: Johns Hopkins University Press, 1957.

Bohlke, L. Brent. *Willa Cather in Person: Interviews, Speeches, and Letters*. Lincoln: University of Nebraska Press, 1986.

Booth, Wayne, *The Rhetoric of Fiction*. Chicago: University of Chicago Press, 1961.

Brewster, William T. *Representative Essays on the Theory of Style*. New York: Macmillan, 1905.

Bronowski, J. *Science and Human Values*. New York: Harper and Son, 1956.

Brooks, Van Wyck. *The Writer in America*. New York: E. P. Dutton, 1953.

Brown, E. K. *Rhythm in the Novel*. Toronto: University of Toronto Press, 1950.

——. *Willa Cather: A Critical Biography*. Completed by Leon Edel. New York: Alfred A. Knopf, 1953.

Brown, Huntington. *Prose Styles: Five Primary Types*. Minneapolis: University of Minnesota Press, 1966.

Brown, Marion Marsh, and Ruth Crone. *Willa Cather: The Woman and Her Works*. New York: Charles Scribner's Sons, 1970.

Brownell, Wm. Craw. *The Genius of Style*. New York: Charles Scribner's Sons, 1924.

Burke, Jack D. *Cell Biology*. Baltimore: Williams and Wilkins, 1970.

Burke, Kenneth. *Langugae As Symbolic Act*. Berkeley: University of California Press, 1966.

Butcher, Fanny. *Many Lives—One Love*. New York: Harper and Row, 1972.

Byrne, Kathleen D., and Richard C. Snyder. *Chrysalis: Willa Cather in Pittsburgh 1896–1906*. Pittsburgh: Historical Society of Western Pennsylvania, 1980.

Callander, Marilyn Berg. *Willa Cather and the Fairy Tale*. Ann Arbor: UMI Research Press, 1989.

Cary, Joyce. *Art and Reality*. New York: Harper Brothers, 1958.

Cather, Willa. *Alexander's Bridge*. Lincoln: University of Nebraska Press, 1977.

———. *A Lost Lady*. New York: Vintage Books, 1972.

———. *Collected Short Fiction*. Introduction by Mildred Bennett. Lincoln: University of Nebraska Press, 1965.

———. *Death Comes for the Archbishop*. New York: Vintage Books, 1971.

———. *Lucy Gayheart*. New York: Alfred A. Knopf, 1935.

———. *My Ántonia*. Boston: Houghton Mifflin, 1954.

———. *My Mortal Enemy*. New York: Vintage Books, 1954.

———. *Not Under Forty*. New York: Alfred A. Knopf, 1964.

———. *On Writing*. New York: Alfred A. Knopf, 1953.

———. *One of Ours*. New York: Vintage Books, 1950.

———. *O Pioneers!*. Boston: Houghton Mifflin, 1941.

———. *The Professor's House*. New York: Vintage Books, 1973.

———. *Sapphira and the Slave Girl*. New York: Vintage Books, 1975.

———. *Shadows on the Rock*. New York: Alfred A. Knopf, 1959.

———. *The Song of the Lark*. Boston: Houghton Mifflin, 1965.

———. *The Troll Garden*. Edited by James Woodress. Lincoln: University of Nebraska Press, 1983.

Coats, Alice M. *Flowers and Their Histories*. New York: McGraw-Hill, 1968.

Coffman, Stanley K., Jr. *Imagism*. Norman: University of Oklahoma Press, 1957.

Commager, Henry Steele. *The American Mind*. New Haven: Yale University Press, 1950.

Cook, David. A. *A History of Narrative Film*. New York: W. W. Norton, 1981.

Cooper, Lane. *Theories of Style*. 1968. Reprint. New York: Burt Franklin, 1907.

Cooperman, Stanley. *World War I and the American Novel*. Baltimore: Johns Hopkins University Press, 1967.

Cowley, Malcolm, ed. *After the Genteel Tradition*. Carbondale: Southern Illinois University Press, 1964.

Craig, David. *The Real Foundations: Literature and Social Change.* New York: Oxford University Press, 1974.

Croce, Benedetto. *Aesthetic as Science of Expression and General Linguistic.* Translated by Douglas Ainsle. London: Macmillan, 1922.

Curtin, William, ed. *The World and the Parish.* Lincoln: University of Nebraska Press, 1970.

Daiches, David. *Willa Cather: A Critical Introduction.* Ithaca: Cornell University Press, 1951.

Dondore, Dorothy Anne. *The Prairie and the Making of America.* New York: Antiquarian, 1961.

Eastman, Max. *The Literary Mind.* New York: Charles Scribner's Sons, 1931.

Edel, Leon. *Willa Cather, The Paradox of Success.* A lecture delivered in 1959. Washington Reference Dept., Library of Congress, 1960.

Eidsvik, Charles. *Cineliteracy: Film among the Arts.* New York: Random House, 1978.

Eliot, T. S. *The Sacred Wood: Essays on Poetry and Criticism.* New York: Alfred A. Knopf, 1920.

Ellmann, Mary. *Thinking about Women.* New York: Harcourt, Brace & World, 1968.

Ellmann, Richard, and Charles Feidelson, Jr., eds., *The Modern Tradition: Backgrounds of Modern Literature.* New York: Oxford University Press, 1965.

Empson, William. *Seven Types of Ambiguity.* London: Chatto and Winders, 1930.

Faulkner, Peter. *Modernism.* London: Methuen, 1977.

Fetterley, Judith. *The Resisting Reader.* Bloomington: Indiana University Press, 1978.

Fickett, Harold and Douglas R. Gilbert. *Flannery O'Connor: Images of Grace.* Grand Rapids, Mich.: William B. Eerdmans, 1986.

Fleishman, Fritz, ed. *American Novelists Revisited: Essays in Feminist Criticism.* Boston: Hall, 1982.

Foerster, Norman. *American Criticism: A Study of Literary Theory from Poe to the Present.* Boston: Houghton Mifflin, 1928.

Ford, Ford Madox. *Return to Yesterday.* London: Victor Gollancz, 1931.

Foss, Martin. *Symbol and Metaphor in Human Experience.* Princeton: Princeton University Press, 1942.

Fowler, Roger, ed. *Style and Structure in Literature: Essays in the New Stylistics.* Ithaca, N.Y.: Cornell University Press, 1975.

Frank, Joseph. *The Widening Gyre: Crisis and Mastery in Modern Literature.* New Brunswick, N.J.: Rutgers University Press, 1963.

Freedman, Richard. *The Novel.* New York: Newsweek Books, 1975.

French, Warren, ed. *The Twenties: Fiction, Poetry, Drama.* Deland, Fla.: Everett Edwards, 1975.

Frye, Northrup. *Anatomy of Criticism: Four Essays.* Princeton: Princeton University Press, 1957.

Geismar, Maxwell. *The Last of the Provincials.* Boston: Houghton Mifflin, 1947.

———. *Rebels and Ancestors.* Boston: Houghton Mifflin, 1953.

Gerber, Philip. *Willa Cather*. Boston: Twayne Publishers, 1975.

Giannetti, Louis. *Understanding Movies*. Englewood Cliffs, N.J.: Prentice-Hall, 1982.

Gianonne, Richard. *Music in Willa Cather's Fiction*. Lincoln: University of Nebraska Press, 1968.

Gibson, Walker. *Tough, Sweet and Stuffy*. Bloomington: Indiana University Press, 1966.

Goldberg, Gerald J., and Nancy M. Goldberg, eds. *The Modern Critical Spectrum*. Englewood Cliffs, N.J.: Prentice-Hall, 1962.

Gordon, Caroline. *How to Read a Novel*. New York: Viking Press, 1957.

Grabo, Carl Henry. *The Technique of the Novel*. New York: Charles Scribner's Sons, 1928.

Graves, Robert, and Alan Hodge. *The Reader over Your Shoulder*. New York: Collier, 1966.

Gurko, Leo. *The Angry Decade*. New York: Dodd, Mead and Company, 1947.

Hardy, Barbara. *The Appropriate Form*. London: Athlowe, 1964.

Hatcher, Harlan. *Creating the Modern American Novel*. New York: Russell & Russell, 1965.

Hazard, Lucy L. *The Frontier in American Literature*. New York: Thomas Y. Crowell, 1927.

Hernadi, Paul. *Beyond Genre: New Directions in Literary Classification*. Ithaca: Cornell University Press, 1972.

Hoffman, Joseph G. *The Life and Death of Cells*. Garden City, N.Y.: Hanover House, 1957.

Hough, Grahm. *Style and Stylistics*. New York: Humanities Press, 1969.

Howe, Irving. *Decline of the New*. New York: Harcourt, Brace & World, 1970.

———. *The Idea of the Modern in Literature and the Arts*. New York: Horizon Press, 1968.

Hughes, Glenn. *Imagism and the Imagists*. Stanford, Calif.: Stanford University Press, 1931.

Hyman, Stanley Edgar. *The Armed Vision: A Study in the Method of Modern Literary Criticism*. New York: Random House, 1955.

Ingarden, Roman, *The Cognition of the Literary Work of Art*. Translated by Ruth Ann Crowley and Kenneth R. Olsen. Evanston, Ill. Northwestern University Press, 1973.

———. *The Literary Work of Art*. Translated by George G. Grabowicz. Evanston, Ill.: Northwestern University Press, 1973.

Iser, Wolfgang. *The Act of Reading*. London: Routledge & Kegan Paul, 1979.

———. *The Implied Reader*. Baltimore: Johns Hopkins University Press, 1974.

Jennings Edward M., ed. *Science and Literature*. Garden City, N.Y.: Doubleday, 1970.

Jessup, Josephine L. *The Faith of Our Feminists*. New York: Richard R. Smith, 1950.

Josipovici, Gabriel. *The Lessons of Modernism*. Totowa, N.J.: Rowman & Littlefield, 1977.

————. *The World and the Book: A Study of Modern Fiction.* Stanford, Calif.: Stanford University Press, 1971.

Kahler, Erich. *The Inward Turn of Narrative.* Translated by R. C. Winston. Princeton, N.J.: 1973.

Kazin, Alfred. *On Native Grounds.* New York: Reynal & Hitchcock, 1942.

Kestner, Joseph A. *The Spatiality of the Novel.* Detroit: Wayne State University Press, 1978.

Knight, Grant C. *The Strenuous Age in American Literature.* Chapel Hill: University of North Carolina Press, 1954.

Koestler, Arthur. *Insight and Outlook.* New York: The Macmillan Company, 1949.

Kugel, James. *The Techniques of Strangeness in Symbolist Poetry.* New Haven: Yale University Press, 1971.

Lawrence, Margaret. *The School of Femininity.* New York: Frederick A. Stokes, 1936.

Lentricchia, Frank. *After the New Criticism.* Chicago: University of Chicago Press, 1980.

Lerner, Laurence, ed. *Reconstructing Literature.* Totowa, N.J.: Barnes & Noble Books, 1983.

LeSage, Laurent. *The French New Novel.* University Park; Pennsylvania State University Press, 1962.

Lewis, Edith. *Willa Cather Living.* New York: Alfred A. Knopf, 1953.

Lubbock, Percy. *The Craft of Fiction.* New York: Peter Smith, 1921.

Macauley, Robie, and George Lanning. *Technique in Fiction.* New York: Harper & Row, 1964.

Mailloux, Steven. *Interpretive Conventions: The Reader in the Study of American Fiction.* Ithaca, N.Y.: Cornell University Press, 1982.

Mainiero, Lina, ed. *American Women Writers.* New York: Frederick Unger, 1979.

McElroy, Davis Dunbar. *Existentialism and Modern Literature.* New York: Philosophical Library, 1963.

Menand, Louis. *Discovering Modernism: T. S. Eliot and His Context.* Oxford: Oxford University Press, 1987.

Miller, James E., Jr. *Quests Surd and Absurd.* Chicago: University of Chicago Press, 1967.

————. *F. Scott Fitzgerald: His Art and His Technique.* New York: New York University Press, 1964.

Miracles of Perception: The Art of Willa Cather. Alderman Library, University of Virginia. Charlottesville: The Library, 1980.

Moers, Ellen. *Literary Women: The Great Writers.* Garden City, N.Y.: Doubleday, 1976.

Monaco, James. *How To Read A Film.* New York: Oxford University Press, 1977.

Muir, Edwin. *The Structure of the Novel.* London: Hogarth Press, 1954.

Munson, Gorham B. *Style and Form in American Prose.* Garden City, N.Y.: Doubleday, Doran & Company, 1929.

Murphy, John J., ed. *Critical Essays on Willa Cather*. Boston: G. K. Hall & Co., 1984.

———, ed. *Five Essays on Willa Cather*. North Andover, Mass.: Merrimack College, 1974.

O'Brien, Sharon. *Willa Cather: The Emerging Voice*. New York: Oxford University Press, 1987.

Olsen, Tillie. *Silences*. New York: Delacorte Press/Seymour Lawrence, 1978.

Ostier, Marianne. *Jewels and the Woman*. New York: Horizon Press, 1958.

Pepper, Stephen C. *The Basis of Criticism in the Arts*. Cambridge: Harvard University Press, 1945.

Pers, Mona. *Willa Cather's Children*. Stockholm, Sweden: Almquist & Wilhsell, Uppsala, 1975.

Phelan, James. *Worlds from Words*. Chicago: University of Chicago Press, 1981.

Porter, Katherine Anne. *The Days Before*. New York: Harcourt, Brace and Company, 1952.

Pratt, Mary Louise. *Toward a Speech Act Theory of Literary Discourse*. Bloomington: Indiana University Press, 1977.

Quinn, Arthur Hobson. *The Literature of the American People*. New York: Appleton-Century-Crofts, 1951.

Quinn, Vernon. *Stories and Legends of Garden Flowers*. New York: Frederick A. Stokes, 1939.

Randall, John H. *The Landscape and the Looking Glass*. Boston: Houghton Mifflin, 1960.

Raban, Jonathan. *The Technique of Modern Fiction: Essays in Practical Criticism*. Notre Dame, Ind.: University of Notre Dame Press, 1969.

Ransom, John Crowe. *The New Criticism*. Norfolk, Conn.: New Directions, 1941.

Rapin, René. *Willa Cather*. New York: R. M. McBride, 1930.

Ray, William. *Literary Meaning: From Phenomenology to Deconstruction*. Oxford: Blackwell, 1984.

Read, Herbert. *The True Voice of Feeling*. New York: Pantheon Books, 1953.

Richards, I. A. *Principles of Literary Criticism*. New York: Harcourt Brace & World, 1925.

———. *Poetries and Sciences*. Reissue of *Science and Poetry*. New York: W. W. Norton, 1970.

Richter, David. *Fable's End: Completeness and Closure in Rhetorical Fiction*. Chicago: University of Chicago Press, 1974.

Robbins, J. Albert, ed. *American Literary Scholarship 1982*. Durham, N.C.: Duke University Press, 1984.

Robinson, Phyllis. *Willa: The Life of Willa Cather*. Garden City, N.Y.: Doubleday, 1983.

Rosowki, Susan J. *The Voyage Perilous: Willa Cather's Romanticism*. Lincoln: University of Nebraska Press, 1986.

Ruternof, Horst. *The Reader's Construction of Narrative*. London: Routledge & Kegan Paul, 1981.

Sacken, Jeanee P. *"A Certain Slant of Light": Aesthetics of First-Person Narration in Gide and Cather.* New York: Garland, 1985.

Schroeter, James, ed. *Willa Cather and Her Critics.* Ithaca, N.Y.: Cornell University Press, 1967.

Sebeak, Thomas, ed. *Style in Language.* Cambridge: Technology Press of Massachusetts Institute of Technology, 1960.

Sergeant, Elizabeth Shepley. *Willa Cather, A Memoir.* Philadelphia: J. B. Lippincott, 1953.

Sheeler, Phillip, and Donald E. Bianchi. *Cell Biology: Structure, Biochemistry, and Function.* New York: John Wiley and Sons, 1983.

Slote, Bernice, ed. *The Kingdom of Art: Willa Cather's First Principles and Critical Statements 1893–1896.* Lincoln: University of Nebraska Press, 1967.

————, and Virginia Faulkner, eds. *The Art of Willa Cather.* Lincoln: University of Nebraska Press, 1974.

Smith, Barbara Hernstein. *On the Margins of Discourse: The Relation of Literature to Language.* Chicago: University of Chicago Press, 1978.

Smith, Henry Nash. *Virgin Land.* Cambridge: Harvard University Press, 1950.

Smitten, Jeffrey R., and Ann Daghistany, eds. *Spatial Form in Narrative.* Ithaca: Cornell University Press, 1981.

Snell, George, *The Shapers of American Fiction.* New York: Cooper Square Publishers, 1961.

Spender, Stephen. *The Struggle of the Modern.* Berkeley: University of California Press, 1963.

Spiegel, Alan. *Fiction and the Camera Eye.* Charlottesville: University of Virginia Press, 1976.

Stallman, Robert Wooster. *Critiques and Essays in Criticism.* New York: Ronald Press, 1949.

Stein, Leo. *Appreciation: Painting, Poetry and Prose.* New York: Crown Publishers, 1947.

Stevens, Wallace. *The Necessary Angel: Essays on Reality and the Imaginations.* New York: Alfred A. Knopf, 1951.

Stevick, Philip. *The Chapter in Fiction.* Syracuse, N.Y.: Syracuse University Press, 1970.

————, ed. *The Theory of the Novel.* New York: Free Press, 1967.

Stouck, David. *Willa Cather's Imagination.* Lincoln: University of Nebraska Press, 1975.

Strelka, Joseph, ed. *Patterns of Literary Style.* University Park: Pennsylvania State University Press, 1971.

Suleiman, Susan, and Inge Crosman. *The Reader in the Text.* Princeton: Princeton University Press, 1980.

Szanto, George. *Narrative Consciousness.* Austin: University of Texas, 1972.

Thorp, Willard. *American Writing in the Twentieth Century.* Cambridge: Harvard University Press, 1960.

Tindall, William York. *The Literary Symbol.* New York: Columbia University Press, 1955.

Todd, Janet, ed. *Gender and Literary Voice.* New York: Holmes and Meier, 1980.

Toliver, Harold. *Animate Illusions: Explorations of Narrative Structure.* Lincoln: University of Nebraska Press, 1974.

Tompkins, Jane P., ed. *Reader-Response Criticism: From Formalism to Post-Structuralism.* Baltimore: Johns Hopkins University Press, 1980.

Torgovnick, Marianna. *Closure in the Novel.* Princeton: Princeton University Press, 1981.

Ullmann, Stephen. *Meaning and Style.* Oxford: Basil Blackwell, 1973.

Urban, Wilbur M. *Language and Reality: The Philosophy of Language and the Principles of Symbolism.* London: G. Allen & Unwin, 1939.

Uzzell, Thomas. *The Technique of the Novel: A Handbook on the Craft of the Long Narrative.* New York: Citadel Press, 1959.

Van Doren, Carl. *The American Novel.* New York: Macmillan, 1940.

Van Ghent, Dorothy. *Willa Cather.* University of Minnesota Pamphlets on American Writers. Minneapolis: University of Minnesota Press, 1964.

Wagenknecht, Edward. *Cavalcade of the American Novel.* New York: Holt, Rinehart and Winston, 1952.

Webster's New World Dictionary of the American Language. Cleveland: World, 1960.

Welty, Eudora. *The Eye of the Story.* New York: Random House, 1977.

Whitehead, Alfred North. *Symbolism: Its Meaning and Effects.* New York: Macmillan, 1927.

Willa Cather: A Pictoral Memoir. Photographs by Lucia Woods and others. Text by Bernice Slote. Lincoln: University of Nebraska Press, 1973.

Wilson, Edmund. *The Shores of Light: A Literary Chronicle of the Twenties and Thirties.* New York: Farrar, Straus, and Young, 1952.

Woodress, James. *Willa Cather: A Literary Life.* Lincoln: University of Nebraska Press, 1987.

——. *Willa Cather: Her Life and Art.* New York: Pegasus, 1970.

Zabel, Morton Davwen. *Craft and Character: Texts, Method, and Vocation in Modern Fiction.* New York: Viking, 1957.

Articles

Adams, Theodore S. "Willa Cather's *My Mortal Enemy*: The Concise Presentation of Scene, Character and Theme." *Colby Library Quarterly* 10 (September 1973): 138–48.

Andersson, Quentin. "Willa Cather: Her Masquerade." *New Republic* 154 (27 November 1965): 28–31.

Arnold, M. "Coming, Willa Cather!" *Women's Studies* 11 (December 1984): 247–60.

Barth, John. "A Few Words About Minimalism." *New York Times Book Review,* 28 December 1986, 1–2, 15.

Bash, James R. "Willa Cather and the Anathema of Materialism." *Colby Library Quarterly* 10 (September 1973): 157–68.

Baym, Max I. "On the Relationship Between Poetry and Science." *Yearbook of Comparative Literature* 5 (1956): 1–5.

———. "Science and Poetry," In *Encyclopedia of Poetry and Poetics*, 743–53. Princeton: Princeton University Press, 1965.

———. "Science is Poetry," *Thought* 45, no. 179 (Winter 1970): 590–600.

Barnes, Hazel. "The Ins and Outs of Robbe-Grillet." *Chicago Review* 15, no. 3 (Winter 1961–62): 21–43.

Barr, Donald. "One Man's Universe." *New York Times*, 21 June 1959, sec. 7, 4.

Benet, Laura. "Review of *The Professor's House.*" *Commonweal* 3 (2 December 1925): 108–9.

Bloom, Lillian, with Edward Bloom. "The Poetics of Willa Cather." In *Five Essays on Willa Cather*, edited by John J. Murphy, 97–119. North Andover, Mass.: Merrimack College, 1974.

Booth, Wayne C. "Distance and Point of View: An Essay in Classification." In *The Theory of the Novel*, edited by Philip Stevick, 87–107. New York: Free Press, 1967.

Brennen, Joseph X. "Willa Cather and Her Music." *University Review* 31 (Spring 1965): 175–83.

———. "Music and Willa Cather." *University Review* 31 (Summer 1965): 257–64.

Brown, E. K. "Homage to Willa Cather." *Yale Review* 36 (Autumn 1946): 77–92.

———. "Willa Cather." In *Willa Cather and Her Critics*, edited by James Schroeter, 72–86. Ithaca, N.Y.: Cornell University Press, 1967.

Bruccoli, Matthew J. "'An Instance of Apparent Plagiarism': F. Scott Fitzgerald, Willa Cather, and the First *Gatsby* Manuscript." *Princeton University Library Chronicle* 39 (1978): 171–78.

Canby, Henry Seidel. "A Novel of the Soul." *Saturday Review* 2 (26 September 1925): 51.

Carroll, Latrobe. "Willa Sibert Cather." *Bookman* 53 (May 1921): 213–16. Reprinted in Bohlke, 19–24.

Cather, Willa. "Nebraska: The End of the First Cycle." *Nation* 117 (5 September 1923): 236–38.

———. Interview with Rose C. Feld. "Restlessness Such as Ours Does Not Make for Beauty." *New York Times*, 21 December 1924, 23. Reprinted in Bohlke, 68–72.

Collins, Jack. "The Literary Endeavor of Willa Cather (As Inspired by Joan Crane's Bibliography)." *Willa Cather Pioneer Memorial Newsletter* 32 (Fall 1988): 33–37.

Comeau, Paul. "Willa Cather's *Lucy Gayheart*: A Long Perspective." *Prairie Schooner* 55 (Spring-Summer 1981): 199–209.

Cousineau, Diane. "Division and Difference in *A Lost Lady*." *Women's Studies* 11 (December 1984), 305–22.

Crosman, Robert. "Do Readers Make Meaning?" In *The Reader in the Text*, edited by Susan Suleiman and Inge Crosman, 149–64. Princeton: Princeton University Press, 1980.

Curtin, William. "Willa Cather: Individualism and Style." *Colby Library Quarterly* 8 (June 1968): 36–58.

Doughty, Howard N., Jr. "Miss Cather as Critic." *Nation* 169 (24 September 1947): 304.

Eichorn, Harry B. "A Falling Out With Love: *My Mortal Enemy.*" *Colby Library Quarterly* 10 (September 1973): 121–38.

Friedman, Norman. "Point of View in Fiction: The Development of a Critical Concept." In *The Theory of the Novel,* edited by Philip Stevick, 108–37. New York: Free Press, 1967.

Gelfant, Blanche H. "The Forgotten Reaping-Hook: Sex in *My Ántonia.*" *American Literature* 43 (March 1971): 60–82.

Geismar, Maxwell. "Willa Cather: Lady in the Wilderness." In *Willa Cather and Her Critics,* edited by James Schroeter, 171–202. Ithaca, N.Y.: Cornell University Press, 1967.

Gerber, Philip. "Willa Cather and The Big Red Rock." *College English* 19 (January 1958): 152–57.

Gish, Robert F. "Paul Hogan and The Biography of Place." *Prairie Schooner* 55 (Spring-Summer 1981): 226–32.

Gitlin, Todd. "Hip-Deep in Post-Modernism." *New York Times Book Review,* 6 November 1988, 1, 35–36.

Greene, George William. "Willa Cather at Mid-Century." *Thought* 32 (Winter 1958): 577–92.

———. "Willa Cather's Grand Manon." *Prairie Schooner* 55 (Spring-Summer 1981): 233–40.

Griffiths, Frederick T. "The Woman Warrior: Willa Cather and *One of Ours.*" *Women's Studies* 11 (December 1984): 261–85.

Grumbach, Doris. "A Study of the Small Room in *The Professor's House.*" *Women's Studies* 11 (December 1984): 327–45.

Hamner, Eugenie Lambert. "The Unknown Well-known Child in Cather's Last Novel." *Women's Studies* 11 (December 1984): 347–57.

Hampton, Benjamin B. "The Author and the Motion Picture." *Bookman* 53 (May 1921): 216–25.

Hays, Peter L. "Hemingway as *Auteur.*" *The South Atlantic Quarterly* 86 (Spring 1987): 151–58.

Heyeck, Robin, and James Woodress. "Willa Cather's Cuts and Revisions in *The Song of the Lark.*" *Modern Fiction Studies* (Winter 1979–80): 651–58.

Hicks, Granville. "The Case Against Willa Cather." In *Willa Cather and Her Critics,* edited by James Schroeter, 139–47. Ithaca, N.Y.: Cornell University Press, 1967.

James, Henry, "The House of Fiction." In *The Theory of the Novel,* edited by Philip Stevick, 58–62. New York: Free Press, 1967.

Jones, Howard Mumford. "The Novels of Willa Cather." *Saturday Review* 18 (6 August 1938): 3–4, 16.

Kahler, Erich. "The Transformation of Modern Fiction." *Comparative Fiction* 7, no. 2 (Spring, 1955): 121–28.

Kramer, Paul J. "Problems in Water Relations of Plants and Cells." In *International Review of Cytology,* edited by G. H. Bourne and J. F. Danielli, assisted by K. W. Jean, 253–86. New York: Academic Press, 1983.

Kronenberger, Louis. "Willa Cather." *Bookman* 74 (October 1931), 134–40.

———. "Willa Cather Fumbles for Another Lost Lady." *New York Times Book Review,* 24 October 1926, 2.

Krutch, Joseph Wood. "Reviews of Four Novels—The Lady as Artist." In *Willa Cather and Her Critics*, edited by James Schroeter, 52–54. Ithaca: Cornell University Press, 1967.

———. "Science and Literature." *Nation* 169 (24 September 1947): 302–3.

Lutwack, Leonard. "Mixed and Uniform Prose Styles in the Novel." In *The Theory of the Novel*, edited by Philip Stevick, 208–19. New York: Free Press, 1967.

Maxfield, J. F. "Strategies of Self-Deception in Willa Cather's *Professor's House*." *Studies in the Novel* 16 (Spring 1984): 72–84.

McGee-Russell, S. M. "The Method of Combined Observations with Light and Electron Microscopes Applied to the Study of Histochemical Colourations in Nerve Cells and Oocytes." In *Cell Structure and Its Interpretations*, by S. M. McGee-Russell and K. F. A. Ross. London: Edward Arnold, 1968.

Moorhead, Elizabeth, "The Novelist." In *Willa Cather and Her Critics*, edited by James Schroeter, 101–13. Ithaca, N.Y.: Cornell University Press, 1967.

Morrow, Nancy. "Willa Cather's *A Lost Lady* and the Nineteenth-century Novel of Adultery." *Women's Studies* 11 (December 1984): 287–303.

Munson, Gorham. B. "Our Postwar Novel." *Bookman* 74 (October 1931): 141–44.

Murphy, John J. "Cooper, Cather and the Downward Path to Progress." *Prairie Schooner* 55 (Spring-Summer 1984): 168–84.

———. "Euripides' *Hippolytus* and Cather's *A Lost Lady*." *American Literature* 53 (March 1981): 72–86.

———. "The Respectable Romantic and The Unwed Mother: Class Consciousness in *My Ántonia*." *Colby Library Quarterly* 10 (September 1973): 149–56.

Murphy, Joseph C. "*Shadows on the Rock* and *To the Lighthouse*—A Bakhtinian Perspective." *Willa Cather Pioneer Memorial Newsletter* 31 (Summer 1987): 31–37.

Noon, W. T. "Modern Literature and the Sense of Time." *Thought* 33, no. 131 (Winter 1958–59): 571–604.

O'Brien, Sharon. "Mothers, Daughters, and the 'Art Necessity': Willa Cather and the Creative Process." In *American Novelists Revisisted: Essays in Feminist Criticism*, edited by Fritz Fleishman, 265–98. Boston: Hall, 1982.

Ohmann, Richard. "Generative Grammars and the Concept of Literary Style." In *Linguistics and Literary Style*, edited by Donald C. Freeman, 258–78. New York: Holt, Rinehart and Winston, 1970.

Pannill, Linda. "Willa Cather's Artist-Heroines." *Women's Studies* 11 (December 1984): 223–32.

Paul, David. "Time and the Novelist." *Partisan Review* 21 (November 1954): 636–49.

Pearson, Norman Holmes. "Willa Cather on Writing." *Saturday Review* 32 (8 October 1949): 37.

Poore, Charles. "The Last Stories of Willa Cather." *New York Times Book Review*, 12 September 1948, 3.

Porter, Katherine Anne. "The Calm, Pure Art of Willa Cather." *New York Times Book Review*, 25 September 1949, 1.

Pound, Ezra. "How to Read." In *Polite Essays*, 155–92. Norfolk, Conn.: New Directions, 1939.

Price, Reynolds. "Men Creating Woman." *New York Times Book Review*, 9 November 1986, 1, 16, 18, 20.

Quirk, Tom. "Fitzgerald and Cather: *The Great Gatsby*." *American Literature* 54 (December 1982): 576–91.

Rose, Phyllis. "Modernism: The Case of Willa Cather." In *Modernism Revisited*, edited by Robert Keily, assisted by John Hildebidle, 123–45. Cambridge: Harvard University Press, 1983.

Rosowski, S. J. "Narrative Technique in Cather's *My Mortal Enemy*." *Journal of Narrative Technique* 8 (Spring 1978): 141–49.

———. "Willa Cather—A Pioneer in Art: *O Pioneers!* and *My Ántonia*." *Prairie Schooner* 55 (Spring-Summer 1981): 141–55.

———. "Willa Cather's Female Landscapes: *The Song of the Lark* and *Lucy Gayheart*." *Women's Studies* 11 (December 1984): 233–46.

Salo, Alice Bell. "*The Professor's House* and *Le Mannequin d'Osier*: A Note on Willa Cather's Narrative Technique." *Studies in American Fiction* 8 (Autumn 1980): 229–31.

Schloss, George. "A Writer's Art." *Hudson Review* 3 (Spring 1950): 151–56.

Scholes, Robert, and Robert Kellogg. "The Problem of Reality: Illustration and Representation." In *The Theory of the Novel*, edited by Philip Stevick. 371–84. New York: Free Press, 1967.

Schorer, Mark. "Technique as Discovery." In *The Theory of the Novel*, edited by Philip Stevick, 65–84. New York: Free Press, 1967.

Schroeter, James. "Willa Cather and *The Professor's House*." *Yale Review* 54 (June 1965): 494–512.

Scott, Fred Newton. "The Most Fundamental Differencia of Poetry and Prose." *PMLA* 19, no. 11 (1904): 250–69.

Seibel, George. "Miss Willa Cather From Nebraska." *New Colophon* (September 1949): 195–209.

Shroder, Maurice Z. "The Noveau Romance and the Tradition of the Novel." *Romantic Review* 17, no. 3 (October 1966), 200–14.

Skaggs, Merrill Maguire. "A Glance into *The Professor's House*: Inward and Outward Bound." *Renascence* 39 (Spring 1987): 422–28.

———. "*Death Comes for the Archbishop*: Cather's Mystery and Manner." *American Literature* 57 (October 1985): 395–406.

———. "*My Mortal Enemy*: Willa Cather's *Tour de Force*." MS.

———. "Poe's Shadow on *Alexander's Bridge*." *Mississippi Quarterly* 35 (Fall 1982): 365–74.

———. "Willa Cather's Experimental Southern Novel." *Mississippi Quarterly* 35, no. 4 (Winter 1981): 3–14.

Slote, Bernice, "Introduction." In *Alexander's Bridge*, by Willa Cather, xxvi. Lincoln: University of Nebraska Press, 1977.

———. "Willa Cather." In *Sixteen Modern American Writers*, edited by Jackson R. Bryer, 29–73. Durham, N.C.: Duke University Press, 1974.

Stierle, Karlheinz. "The Reading of Fictional Texts." In *The Reader in the Text*, edited by Susan Suleiman and Inge Crosman, 83–105. Princeton: Princeton University Press, 1980.

Stofer, Kathryn T. "Gems and Jewelry: Cather's Imagery in *My Mortal Enemy.*" *Willa Cather Pioneer Memorial Newsletter* 30 (Summer 1986), 19–22.

Trilling, Lionel. "Willa Cather." In *After the Genteel Tradition*, edited by Malcolm Cowley, 48–56. Carbondale: Southern Illinois University Press, 1964.

———. "Willa Cather." In *Willa Cather and Her Critics*, edited by James Schroeter, 148–55. Ithaca, N.Y.: Cornell University Press, 1967.

Wagner, Linda W. "Tension and Technique: The Years of Greatness." *Studies in American Fiction* 5 (1977): 64–77.

Wellworth, G. E. "Life in the Void." *University of Kansas City Review* 28, no. 2 (October 1961): 25–33.

West, Rebecca. "The Classic Artist." In *Willa Cather and Her Critics*, edited by James Schroeter, 62–71. Ithaca, N.Y.: Cornell University Press, 1967.

Wild, Barbara, "'The Thing Not Named' in *The Professor's House.*" *Western American Literature* 12 (1978): 263–74.

Wilson, Edmund. "Two Novels of Willa Cather." In *Willa Cather and Her Critics*, edited by James Schroeter, 25–29. Ithaca, N.Y.: Cornell University Press, 1967.

Winsten, Archer. "A Defense of Willa Cather." *Bookman* 74 (March 1932): 634–41.

Zabel, Morton Davwen. "Willa Cather." *Nation* 164 (14 June 1947): 713–16.

Dissertations

Callander, Marilyn Berg. "Willa Cather's Use of Fairy Tales." Ph.D. diss., Drew University, 1987.

Cassai, Mary Ann. "Symbolic Techniques in Selected Novels of Willa Cather." Ph.D. diss., New York University, 1978.

Doughaday, Charles H. "Willa Cather's 'Happy Experimenting': Artistic Fusion of Theme and Structure." Ph.D. diss., University of Kentucky, 1967.

Lambert, Maude Eugenie. "Theme and Craftsmanship in Willa Cather's Novels." Ph.D. diss., University of North Carolina, 1965.

Massey, David G. "Simplicity With Suggestiveness in Willa Cather's Revised and Republished Fiction." Ph.D. diss., Drew University, 1979.

Moseley, Ann. "The Voyage Perilous: Willa Cather's Mythic Quest." Ph.D. diss., University of Oklahoma, 1974.

Schmittlein, Albert Edward. "Willa Cather's Novels: An Evolving Art." Ph.D. diss., University of Pittsburgh, 1962.

Throckmorton, Jean Lavon. "Willa Cather: Artistic Theory and Practice (Volumes 1 and 2)." Ph.D. diss., University of Kansas, 1954.

Whittington, Charles Calvin, Jr. "The Use of Insert Narrative in the Novels of Willa Cather." Ph.D. diss., Vanderbilt University, 1972.

Yongue, Patricia Lee. "The Immense Design: A Study of Willa Cather's Creative Process." Ph.D. diss., University of California at Los Angeles, 1972.

Index